DEAR FUTURE EXAM SUCCESS STORY

First of all, **THANK YOU** for purchasing Mometrix study materials!

Second, congratulations! You are one of the few determined test-takers who are committed to doing whatever it takes to excel on your exam. **You have come to the right place.** We developed these study materials with one goal in mind: to deliver you the information you need in a format that's concise and easy to use.

In addition to optimizing your guide for the content of the test, we've outlined our recommended steps for breaking down the preparation process into small, attainable goals so you can make sure you stay on track.

We've also analyzed the entire test-taking process, identifying the most common pitfalls and showing how you can overcome them and be ready for any curveball the test throws you.

Standardized testing is one of the biggest obstacles on your road to success, which only increases the importance of doing well in the high-pressure, high-stakes environment of test day. Your results on this test could have a significant impact on your future, and this guide provides the information and practical advice to help you achieve your full potential on test day.

Your success is our success

We would love to hear from you! If you would like to share the story of your exam success or if you have any questions or comments in regard to our products, please contact us at **800-673-8175** or **support@mometrix.com**.

Thanks again for your business and we wish you continued success!

Sincerely,
The Mometrix Test Preparation Team

I0894307

Written and edited by the Mometrix Test Preparation Team
Printed in the United States of America

Mometrix
TEST PREPARATION

MCA

Success Strategies
Grade 8
Science

TABLE OF CONTENTS

INTRODUCTION 1

STRATEGY #1 – PLAN BIG, STUDY SMALL 2

STRATEGY #2 – MAKE YOUR STUDYING COUNT 3

STRATEGY #3 – PRACTICE THE RIGHT WAY 4

STRATEGY #4 – PACE YOURSELF 6

TEST-TAKING STRATEGIES 7

SCIENCE 11

- SCIENTIFIC INVESTIGATION AND REASONING 11
- MATTER AND ENERGY 22
- FORCE, MOTION, AND ENERGY 39
- EARTH AND SPACE SCIENCE 49
- ORGANISMS AND ENVIRONMENTS 67

PRACTICE TEST #1 95

ANSWER KEY AND EXPLANATIONS 106

PRACTICE TEST #2 112

ANSWER KEY AND EXPLANATIONS 123

HOW TO OVERCOME TEST ANXIETY 129

THANK YOU 135

ONLINE RESOURCES 136

Introduction

Thank you for purchasing this resource! You have made the choice to prepare yourself for a test that could have a huge impact on your future, and this guide is designed to help you be fully ready for test day. Obviously, it's important to have a solid understanding of the test material, but you also need to be prepared for the unique environment and stressors of the test, so that you can perform to the best of your abilities.

For this purpose, the first section that appears in this guide is the **Success Strategies**. We've devoted countless hours to meticulously researching what works and what doesn't, and we've boiled down our findings to the most impactful steps you can take to improve your performance on the test. We start at the beginning with study planning and move through the preparation process, all the way to the testing strategies that will help you get the most out of what you know when you're finally sitting in front of the test.

We recommend that you start preparing for your test as far in advance as possible. However, if you've bought this guide as a last-minute study resource and only have a few days before your test, we recommend that you skip over the first two Success Strategies since they address a long-term study plan.

If you struggle with **test anxiety**, we strongly encourage you to check out our recommendations for how you can overcome it. Test anxiety is a formidable foe, but it can be beaten, and we want to make sure you have the tools you need to defeat it.

Strategy #1 – Plan Big, Study Small

There's a lot riding on your performance. If you want to ace this test, you're going to need to keep your skills sharp and the material fresh in your mind. You need a plan that lets you review everything you need to know while still fitting in your schedule. We'll break this strategy down into three categories.

Information Organization

Start with the information you already have: the official test outline. From this, you can make a complete list of all the concepts you need to cover before the test. Organize these concepts into groups that can be studied together, and create a list of any related vocabulary you need to learn so you can brush up on any difficult terms. You'll want to keep this vocabulary list handy once you actually start studying since you may need to add to it along the way.

Time Management

Once you have your set of study concepts, decide how to spread them out over the time you have left before the test. Break your study plan into small, clear goals so you have a manageable task for each day and know exactly what you're doing. Then just focus on one small step at a time. When you manage your time this way, you don't need to spend hours at a time studying. Studying a small block of content for a short period each day helps you retain information better and avoid stressing over how much you have left to do. You can relax knowing that you have a plan to cover everything in time. In order for this strategy to be effective though, you have to start studying early and stick to your schedule. Avoid the exhaustion and futility that comes from last-minute cramming!

Study Environment

The environment you study in has a big impact on your learning. Studying in a coffee shop, while probably more enjoyable, is not likely to be as fruitful as studying in a quiet room. It's important to keep distractions to a minimum. You're only planning to study for a short block of time, so make the most of it. Don't pause to check your phone or get up to find a snack. It's also important to **avoid multitasking**. Research has consistently shown that multitasking will make your studying dramatically less effective. Your study area should also be comfortable and well-lit so you don't have the distraction of straining your eyes or sitting on an uncomfortable chair.

The time of day you study is also important. You want to be rested and alert. Don't wait until just before bedtime. Study when you'll be most likely to comprehend and remember. Even better, if you know what time of day your test will be, set that time aside for study. That way your brain will be used to working on that subject at that specific time and you'll have a better chance of recalling information.

Finally, it can be helpful to team up with others who are studying for the same test. Your actual studying should be done in as isolated an environment as possible, but the work of organizing the information and setting up the study plan can be divided up. In between study sessions, you can discuss with your teammates the concepts that you're all studying and quiz each other on the details. Just be sure that your teammates are as serious about the test as you are. If you find that your study time is being replaced with social time, you might need to find a new team.

Strategy #2 – Make Your Studying Count

You're devoting a lot of time and effort to preparing for this test, so you want to be absolutely certain it will pay off. This means doing more than just reading the content and hoping you can remember it on test day. It's important to make every minute of study count. There are two main areas you can focus on to make your studying count.

Retention

It doesn't matter how much time you study if you can't remember the material. You need to make sure you are retaining the concepts. To check your retention of the information you're learning, try recalling it at later times with minimal prompting. Try carrying around flashcards and glance at one or two from time to time or ask a friend who's also studying for the test to quiz you.

To enhance your retention, look for ways to put the information into practice so that you can apply it rather than simply recalling it. If you're using the information in practical ways, it will be much easier to remember. Similarly, it helps to solidify a concept in your mind if you're not only reading it to yourself but also explaining it to someone else. Ask a friend to let you teach them about a concept you're a little shaky on (or speak aloud to an imaginary audience if necessary). As you try to summarize, define, give examples, and answer your friend's questions, you'll understand the concepts better and they will stay with you longer. Finally, step back for a big picture view and ask yourself how each piece of information fits with the whole subject. When you link the different concepts together and see them working together as a whole, it's easier to remember the individual components.

Finally, practice showing your work on any multi-step problems, even if you're just studying. Writing out each step you take to solve a problem will help solidify the process in your mind, and you'll be more likely to remember it during the test.

Modality

Modality simply refers to the means or method by which you study. Choosing a study modality that fits your own individual learning style is crucial. No two people learn best in exactly the same way, so it's important to know your strengths and use them to your advantage.

For example, if you learn best by visualization, focus on visualizing a concept in your mind and draw an image or a diagram. Try color-coding your notes, illustrating them, or creating symbols that will trigger your mind to recall a learned concept. If you learn best by hearing or discussing information, find a study partner who learns the same way or read aloud to yourself. Think about how to put the information in your own words. Imagine that you are giving a lecture on the topic and record yourself so you can listen to it later.

For any learning style, flashcards can be helpful. Organize the information so you can take advantage of spare moments to review. Underline key words or phrases. Use different colors for different categories. Mnemonic devices (such as creating a short list in which every item starts with the same letter) can also help with retention. Find what works best for you and use it to store the information in your mind most effectively and easily.

Strategy #3 – Practice the Right Way

Your success on test day depends not only on how many hours you put into preparing, but also on whether you prepared the right way. It's good to check along the way to see if your studying is paying off. One of the most effective ways to do this is by taking practice tests to evaluate your progress. Practice tests are useful because they show exactly where you need to improve. Every time you take a practice test, pay special attention to these three groups of questions:

- The questions you got wrong
- The questions you had to guess on, even if you guessed right
- The questions you found difficult or slow to work through

This will show you exactly what your weak areas are, and where you need to devote more study time. Ask yourself why each of these questions gave you trouble. Was it because you didn't understand the material? Was it because you didn't remember the vocabulary? Do you need more repetitions on this type of question to build speed and confidence? Dig into those questions and figure out how you can strengthen your weak areas as you go back to review the material.

Additionally, many practice tests have a section explaining the answer choices. It can be tempting to read the explanation and think that you now have a good understanding of the concept. However, an explanation likely only covers part of the question's broader context. Even if the explanation makes perfect sense, **go back and investigate** every concept related to the question until you're positive you have a thorough understanding.

As you go along, keep in mind that the practice test is just that: practice. Memorizing these questions and answers will not be very helpful on the actual test because it is unlikely to have any of the same exact questions. If you only know the right answers to the sample questions, you won't be prepared for the real thing. **Study the concepts** until you understand them fully, and then you'll be able to answer any question that shows up on the test.

It's important to wait on the practice tests until you're ready. If you take a test on your first day of study, you may be overwhelmed by the amount of material covered and how much you need to learn. Work up to it gradually.

On test day, you'll need to be prepared for answering questions, managing your time, and using the test-taking strategies you've learned. It's a lot to balance, like a mental marathon that will have a big impact on your future. Like training for a marathon, you'll need to start slowly and work your way up. When test day arrives, you'll be ready.

Start with the strategies you've read in the first two Success Strategies—plan your course and study in the way that works best for you. If you have time, consider using multiple study resources to get different approaches to the same concepts. It can be helpful to see difficult concepts from more than one angle. Then find a good source for practice tests. Many times, the test website will suggest potential study resources or provide sample tests.

Practice Test Strategy

If you're able to find at least three practice tests, we recommend this strategy:

Untimed and Open-Book Practice

Take the first test with no time constraints and with your notes and study guide handy. Take your time and focus on applying the strategies you've learned.

Timed and Open-Book Practice

Take the second practice test open-book as well, but set a timer and practice pacing yourself to finish in time.

Timed and Closed-Book Practice

Take any other practice tests as if it were test day. Set a timer and put away your study materials. Sit at a table or desk in a quiet room, imagine yourself at the testing center, and answer questions as quickly and accurately as possible.

Keep repeating timed and closed-book tests on a regular basis until you run out of practice tests or it's time for the actual test. Your mind will be ready for the schedule and stress of test day, and you'll be able to focus on recalling the material you've learned.

Strategy #4 – Pace Yourself

Once you're fully prepared for the material on the test, your biggest challenge on test day will be managing your time. Just knowing that the clock is ticking can make you panic even if you have plenty of time left. Work on pacing yourself so you can build confidence against the time constraints of the exam. Pacing is a difficult skill to master, especially in a high-pressure environment, so **practice is vital**.

Set time expectations for your pace based on how much time is available. For example, if a section has 60 questions and the time limit is 30 minutes, you know you have to average 30 seconds or less per question in order to answer them all. Although 30 seconds is the hard limit, set 25 seconds per question as your goal, so you reserve extra time to spend on harder questions. When you budget extra time for the harder questions, you no longer have any reason to stress when those questions take longer to answer.

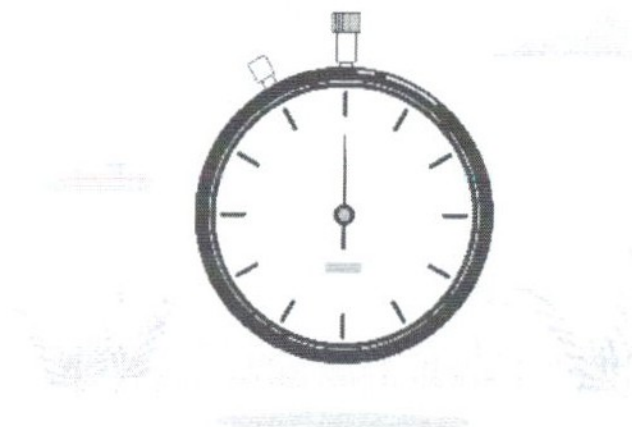

Don't let this time expectation distract you from working through the test at a calm, steady pace, but keep it in mind so you don't spend too much time on any one question. Recognize that taking extra time on one question you don't understand may keep you from answering two that you do understand later in the test. If your time limit for a question is up and you're still not sure of the answer, mark it and move on, and come back to it later if the time and the test format allow. If the testing format doesn't allow you to return to earlier questions, just make an educated guess; then put it out of your mind and move on.

On the easier questions, be careful not to rush. It may seem wise to hurry through them so you have more time for the challenging ones, but it's not worth missing one if you know the concept and just didn't take the time to read the question fully. Work efficiently but make sure you understand the question and have looked at all of the answer choices, since more than one may seem right at first.

Even if you're paying attention to the time, you may find yourself a little behind at some point. You should speed up to get back on track, but do so wisely. Don't panic; just take a few seconds less on each question until you're caught up. Don't guess without thinking, but do look through the answer choices and eliminate any you know are wrong. If you can get down to two choices, it is often worthwhile to guess from those. Once you've chosen an answer, move on and don't dwell on any that you skipped or had to hurry through. If a question was taking too long, chances are it was one of the harder ones, so you weren't as likely to get it right anyway.

On the other hand, if you find yourself getting ahead of schedule, it may be beneficial to slow down a little. The more quickly you work, the more likely you are to make a careless mistake that will affect your score. You've budgeted time for each question, so don't be afraid to spend that time. Practice an efficient but careful pace to get the most out of the time you have.

Test-Taking Strategies

This section contains a list of test-taking strategies that you may find helpful as you work through the test. By taking what you know and applying logical thought, you can maximize your chances of answering any question correctly!

It is very important to realize that every question is different and every person is different: no single strategy will work on every question, and no single strategy will work for every person. That's why we've included all of them here, so you can try them out and determine which ones work best for different types of questions and which ones work best for you.

Question Strategies

☑ Read Carefully

Read the question and the answer choices carefully. Don't miss the question because you misread the terms. You have plenty of time to read each question thoroughly and make sure you understand what is being asked. Yet a happy medium must be attained, so don't waste too much time. You must read carefully and efficiently.

☑ Contextual Clues

Look for contextual clues. If the question includes a word you are not familiar with, look at the immediate context for some indication of what the word might mean. Contextual clues can often give you all the information you need to decipher the meaning of an unfamiliar word. Even if you can't determine the meaning, you may be able to narrow down the possibilities enough to make a solid guess at the answer to the question.

☑ Prefixes

If you're having trouble with a word in the question or answer choices, try dissecting it. Take advantage of every clue that the word might include. Prefixes can be a huge help. Usually, they allow you to determine a basic meaning. *Pre-* means before, *post-* means after, *pro-* is positive, *de-* is negative. From prefixes, you can get an idea of the general meaning of the word and try to put it into context.

☑ Hedge Words

Watch out for critical hedge words, such as *likely, may, can, often, almost, mostly, usually, generally, rarely*, and *sometimes*. Question writers insert these hedge phrases to cover every possibility. Often an answer choice will be wrong simply because it leaves no room for exception. Be on guard for answer choices that have definitive words such as *exactly* and *always*.

☑ Switchback Words

Stay alert for *switchbacks*. These are the words and phrases frequently used to alert you to shifts in thought. The most common switchback words are *but, although*, and *however*. Others include *nevertheless, on the other hand, even though, while, in spite of, despite*, and *regardless of*. Switchback words are important to catch because they can change the direction of the question or an answer choice.

⊘ Face Value

When in doubt, use common sense. Accept the situation in the problem at face value. Don't read too much into it. These problems will not require you to make wild assumptions. If you have to go beyond creativity and warp time or space in order to have an answer choice fit the question, then you should move on and consider the other answer choices. These are normal problems rooted in reality. The applicable relationship or explanation may not be readily apparent, but it is there for you to figure out. Use your common sense to interpret anything that isn't clear.

Answer Choice Strategies

⊘ Answer Selection

The most thorough way to pick an answer choice is to identify and eliminate wrong answers until only one is left, then confirm it is the correct answer. Sometimes an answer choice may immediately seem right, but be careful. The test writers will usually put more than one reasonable answer choice on each question, so take a second to read all of them and make sure that the other choices are not equally obvious. As long as you have time left, it is better to read every answer choice than to pick the first one that looks right without checking the others.

⊘ Answer Choice Families

An answer choice family consists of two (in rare cases, three) answer choices that are very similar in construction and cannot all be true at the same time. If you see two answer choices that are direct opposites or parallels, one of them is usually the correct answer. For instance, if one answer choice says that quantity *x* increases and another either says that quantity *x* decreases (opposite) or says that quantity *y* increases (parallel), then those answer choices would fall into the same family. An answer choice that doesn't match the construction of the answer choice family is more likely to be incorrect. Most questions will not have answer choice families, but when they do appear, you should be prepared to recognize them.

⊘ Eliminate Answers

Eliminate answer choices as soon as you realize they are wrong, but make sure you consider all possibilities. If you are eliminating answer choices and realize that the last one you are left with is also wrong, don't panic. Start over and consider each choice again. There may be something you missed the first time that you will realize on the second pass.

⊘ Avoid Fact Traps

Don't be distracted by an answer choice that is factually true but doesn't answer the question. You are looking for the choice that answers the question. Stay focused on what the question is asking for so you don't accidentally pick an answer that is true but incorrect. Always go back to the question and make sure the answer choice you've selected actually answers the question and is not merely a true statement.

⊘ Extreme Statements

In general, you should avoid answers that put forth extreme actions as standard practice or proclaim controversial ideas as established fact. An answer choice that states the "process should be used in certain situations, if..." is much more likely to be correct than one that states the "process should be discontinued completely." The first is a calm rational statement and doesn't even make a definitive, uncompromising stance, using a hedge word *if* to provide wiggle room, whereas the second choice is far more extreme.

⊘ BENCHMARK

As you read through the answer choices and you come across one that seems to answer the question well, mentally select that answer choice. This is not your final answer, but it's the one that will help you evaluate the other answer choices. The one that you selected is your benchmark or standard for judging each of the other answer choices. Every other answer choice must be compared to your benchmark. That choice is correct until proven otherwise by another answer choice beating it. If you find a better answer, then that one becomes your new benchmark. Once you've decided that no other choice answers the question as well as your benchmark, you have your final answer.

⊘ PREDICT THE ANSWER

Before you even start looking at the answer choices, it is often best to try to predict the answer. When you come up with the answer on your own, it is easier to avoid distractions and traps because you will know exactly what to look for. The right answer choice is unlikely to be word-for-word what you came up with, but it should be a close match. Even if you are confident that you have the right answer, you should still take the time to read each option before moving on.

General Strategies

⊘ TOUGH QUESTIONS

If you are stumped on a problem or it appears too hard or too difficult, don't waste time. Move on! Remember though, if you can quickly check for obviously incorrect answer choices, your chances of guessing correctly are greatly improved. Before you completely give up, at least try to knock out a couple of possible answers. Eliminate what you can and then guess at the remaining answer choices before moving on.

⊘ CHECK YOUR WORK

Since you will probably not know every term listed and the answer to every question, it is important that you get credit for the ones that you do know. Don't miss any questions through careless mistakes. If at all possible, try to take a second to look back over your answer selection and make sure you've selected the correct answer choice and haven't made a costly careless mistake (such as marking an answer choice that you didn't mean to mark). This quick double check should more than pay for itself in caught mistakes for the time it costs.

⊘ PACE YOURSELF

It's easy to be overwhelmed when you're looking at a page full of questions; your mind is confused and full of random thoughts, and the clock is ticking down faster than you would like. Calm down and maintain the pace that you have set for yourself. Especially as you get down to the last few minutes of the test, don't let the small numbers on the clock make you panic. As long as you are on track by monitoring your pace, you are guaranteed to have time for each question.

⊘ DON'T RUSH

It is very easy to make errors when you are in a hurry. Maintaining a fast pace in answering questions is pointless if it makes you miss questions that you would have gotten right otherwise. Test writers like to include distracting information and wrong answers that seem right. Taking a little extra time to avoid careless mistakes can make all the difference in your test score. Find a pace that allows you to be confident in the answers that you select.

✓ Keep Moving

Panicking will not help you pass the test, so do your best to stay calm and keep moving. Taking deep breaths and going through the answer elimination steps you practiced can help to break through a stress barrier and keep your pace.

Final Notes

The combination of a solid foundation of content knowledge and the confidence that comes from practicing your plan for applying that knowledge is the key to maximizing your performance on test day. As your foundation of content knowledge is built up and strengthened, you'll find that the strategies included in this chapter become more and more effective in helping you quickly sift through the distractions and traps of the test to isolate the correct answer.

Now that you're preparing to move forward into the test content chapters of this book, be sure to keep your goal in mind. As you read, think about how you will be able to apply this information on the test. If you've already seen sample questions for the test and you have an idea of the question format and style, try to come up with questions of your own that you can answer based on what you're reading. This will give you valuable practice applying your knowledge in the same ways you can expect to on test day.

Good luck and good studying!

Science

Scientific Investigation and Reasoning

Safety Procedures

Everyone working in a lab setting should be careful to follow these rules to protect themselves and others from injury or accidents.

- Students should wear a **lab apron** and **safety goggles**.
- **Loose** or **dangling** clothing and jewelry, necklaces, and earrings should not be worn.
- Those with **long hair** should tie it back.
- Care should always be taken not to **splash chemicals**.
- **Open-toed shoes** such as sandals and flip-flops should not be worn, nor should wrist watches.
- **Glasses** are preferable to contact lenses since the latter carries a risk of chemicals getting caught between the lens and the eye.
- Students should always be **supervised** during an experiment.
- The area where the experiment is taking place and the surrounding floor should be **free of clutter**.
- **Food** and **drink** should also not be allowed in a lab setting.
- **Cords** should not be allowed to **dangle** from work stations.
- There should be no **rough-housing** in the lab.
- **Wash hands** before and after the lab is complete.

Safety Gloves

There are many types of **gloves** available to help protect the skin from cuts, burns, and chemical splashes. There are many considerations to take into account when choosing a glove. For example, gloves that are highly protective may limit grip or accuracy. Some gloves may not offer appropriate protection against a specific chemical. Disposable latex, vinyl, or nitrile gloves are usually appropriate for most circumstances, and offer protection from incidental splashes and contact.

Laboratory Accidents

Accidents happen in labs, so it is important to know how to clean up, stay safe, and report the accident to the teacher. Any spills or accidents should be **reported** to the teacher so that the teacher can determine the safest clean-up method. The student should start to wash off a **chemical** spilled on the skin while reporting the incident. Some spills may require removal of contaminated clothing and use of the **safety shower**. Broken glass should be disposed of in a designated container. If someone's clothing catches fire they should walk to the safety shower and use it to extinguish the flames. A fire blanket may be used to smother a **lab fire**. A fire extinguisher, phone, spill neutralizers, and a first aid box are other types of **safety equipment** found in the lab. Students should be familiar with **routes** out of the room and the building in case of fire.

Natural Resources, Renewable Resources, Nonrenewable Resources, and Commodities

Natural resources are things provided by nature that have value to humans, such as minerals, energy, timber, fish, wildlife, and the landscape. **Renewable resources** are those that can be replenished, such as wind, solar radiation, tides, and water (with proper conservation and cleanup). Soil is renewable with proper conservation and management techniques, and timber can be replenished with replanting. Living resources such as fish and wildlife can replenish themselves if they are not over-harvested. **Nonrenewable resources** are those that cannot be replenished. These include fossil fuels such as oil and coal and metal ores. These cannot be replaced or reused once they have been burned, although some of their products can be recycled. **Commodities** are natural resources that have to be extracted and purified rather than created, such as mineral ores.

Recycling and Protecting the Environment

When trash is thrown away without separating it out for recycling, it usually goes to a landfill where it cannot be recovered and reused. Metal and plastic do not break down readily, and by sending those to the general trash, those materials are essentially lost. Aluminum cans, like soda cans and canned foods can be recycled and used to make new products down the line. The same can be said of most paper and plastics. Recycling bins are usually next to normal trash cans and have the recycle symbol marked on it. This is usually three arrows pointing at each other in a triangle:

Definition of Science

Scientific knowledge is knowledge about the world that we understand by observing and testing. The **scientific process** is how we try to gain scientific knowledge. The steps are to make an initial observation, make a hypothesis, test the hypothesis with an experiment, draw conclusions from the experiment, then start over with new observations.

Observations

An **observation** is something specific you notice about the world or an event. For instance, a very obvious event that takes place is if we leave milk out on the counter overnight, the milk will go bad. We observe this event by using our five senses: sight, taste, smell, touch, and sound. When milk goes bad, there are several ways it changes.

Hypothesis

The next step of the scientific process is to make an educated guess about what might happen in a certain event. This is also known as a **hypothesis**. A hypothesis about milk might be that if I keep milk above a certain temperature for a long time, it will go bad. Hypotheses need to be specific and testable so we can decide if it is true or false.

Experiment

The step after making a hypothesis is to check if it is true by testing it with an **experiment**. Experiments need to be a controlled, specific situation that tells us if our educated guess was correct. Experiments need to ask questions about **facts**, rather than **opinions**. Usually, the more specific the experiment, the clearer the answer will be. For instance, if I test my hypothesis by putting milk outside overnight, but do not set a timer, then I can get an answer, but I will not be able to record how time affected the experiment. Similarly, if the milk is outside and the temperature changes overnight, I will not be able to learn much about what effect the temperature had on the milk.

Variables

These two aspects of the experiment are examples of variables. **Variables** are parts of the experiment that can change. Some variables are controlled, while others are aspects that we observe. For instance, we cannot control time, but we can observe the milk over time by checking it every half hour. Temperature, on the other hand, can be controlled with technology. We can keep the milk inside the house, where the temperature will always be around 70 degrees, or we can keep it in the refrigerator, where the milk will stay close to 40 degrees. These variables need to be controlled as best as possible to get the most specific results.

Repeating Experiments

Experiments should be **repeated** to see if the same result happens every time. For example, if you can get the same result only three out of ten attempts, then the result is not reliable and the experiment should be changed and tried again. Another example is that if you are testing how milk changes by setting it out, try changing the temperature each time to see if the same result happens at different temperatures.

Reflect

After an experiment is complete, the scientist needs to **reflect** on what happened by asking questions:

- Did the experiment answer the question?
- Was the hypothesis true or false?
- Did repeated attempts produce the same results?
- Is there anything I should change for future attempts?
- What did I learn?
- What questions can I ask now that I have learned something?

Repeat the Process

After the experiment and reflection is over, the scientist hopefully learned something and can ask new questions. These questions should be more specific, or the experiment should be improved to get better answers.

Observed and Measured Data

Data can be either measurable or observable. **Observable data** is often referred to as **qualitative data**, because it describes specific **qualities** of something being observed. An example of this is color or smell. It is very difficult to find numbers to describe a color or smell, but it is not hard to describe that a liquid changed from red to blue. **Measurable data** is also known as **quantitative data** because it refers to the quantity or amount of something. A good example of quantitative data is weight. Any time someone steps on a scale to know how much they weigh, they are looking at quantitative data. Both types of data are important to keep track of and record.

Metric and International System of Units

The **metric system** is the accepted standard of measurement in the scientific community. The **International System of Units (SI)** is a set of measurements (including the metric system) that is almost globally accepted. The United States, Liberia, and Myanmar have not accepted this system. **Standardization** is important because it allows the results of experiments to be compared and reproduced without the need to laboriously convert measurements. The SI is based partially on the **meter-kilogram-second (MKS) system** rather than the **centimeter-gram-second (CGS) system**. The MKS system considers meters, kilograms, and seconds to be the basic units of measurement, while the CGS system considers centimeters, grams, and seconds to be the basic units of measurement. Under the MKS system, the length of an object would be expressed as 1 meter instead of 100 centimeters, which is how it would be described under the CGS system.

Review Video: Metric System Conversions
Visit mometrix.com/academy and enter code: 163709

Metric System

The **metric system** is the accepted standard of measurement in the scientific community. **Standardization** is helpful because it allows the results of experiments to be compared and reproduced without the need to laboriously convert measurements. Metric system uses similar conversions between all types of measurement, including length, mass, volume, time, and temperature.

English and Metric (Scientific) Units of Measurement

The English system commonly used in the United States is not based on consistent smaller units. Thus, 12 inches equal 1 foot, 3 feet equal 1 yard, and 5,280 feet equal 1 mile. The metric system used in science and most countries of the world is based on units of 10. Therefore, 1000 millimeters and 100 centimeters equal 1 meter, and 1,000 meters equal a kilometer. The same pattern is true for the other units of measurement in the two systems. The following table shows the different units.

Unit	English System	Metric System
length	inch, foot, mile	centimeter, meter, kilometer
mass, weight	net weight ounce, pound	gram, kilogram, newton
volume	fluid ounce, pint, quart	milliliter, liter
temperature	Fahrenheit degree	Celsius degree

Fahrenheit and Celsius Temperature Scales

In the Fahrenheit scale the point where water freezes and ice melts is set at 32°, and the point where water boils and water vapor condenses is 212°. That means a difference of 180° between the freezing and boiling points of water. In the Celsius scale, the freezing/melting point is set at 0°and the boiling/condensation point at 100°, making this scale much easier to use.

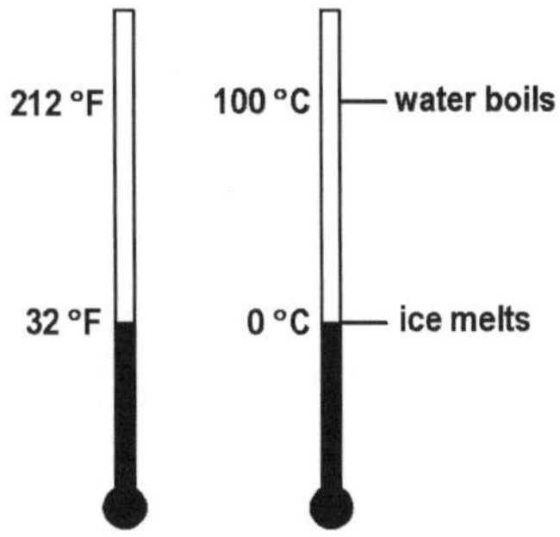

Basic Units of Measurement

Using the **metric system** is generally accepted as the preferred method for taking measurements. Having a **universal standard** allows individuals to interpret measurements more easily, regardless of where they are located. The basic units of measurement are: the **meter**, which measures length; the **liter**, which measures volume; and the **gram**, which measures mass. The metric system starts with a base unit and increases or decreases in units of 10. The prefix and the base unit combined are used to indicate an amount. For example, deka- is 10 times the base unit. A dekameter is 10 meters; a dekaliter is 10 liters; and a dekagram is 10 grams. The prefix hecto- refers to 100 times the base amount; kilo- is 1,000 times the base amount. The prefixes that indicate a fraction of the base unit are deci-, which is 1/10 of the base unit; centi-, which is 1/100 of the base unit; and milli-, which is 1/1000 of the base unit.

Common Prefixes

The prefixes for **multiples** are as follows:

deka	(da)	10 (deka is the American spelling, but deca is also used)
hecto	(h)	100
kilo	(k)	1,000
mega	(M)	100,000

The prefixes for **subdivisions** are as follows:

deci	(d)	1/10
centi	(c)	1/100
milli	(m)	1/1,000
micro	(μ)	1/100,000

Venn Diagrams

One helpful way of sorting out information when comparing two things is a **venn diagram.** This tool is essentially just two circles that overlap, and it is used to display what aspects of one thing are similar or different from another thing. In the following diagram, notice how fish and frogs are similar in some ways, but different in others.

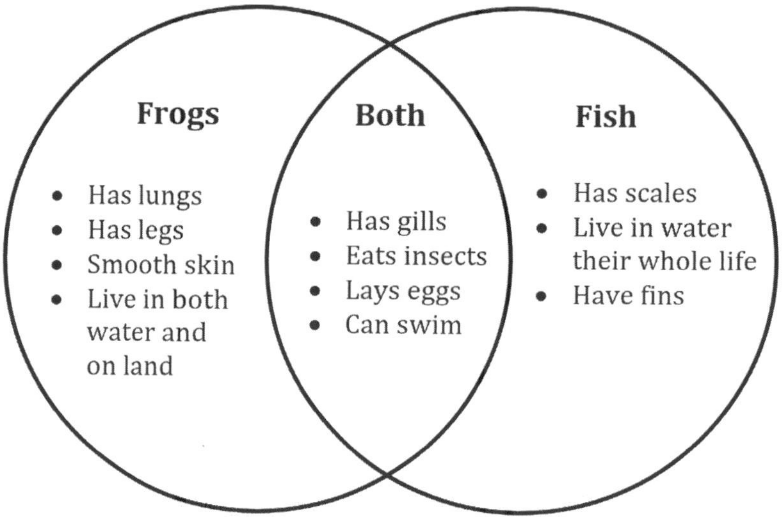

Frequency Tables

Frequency tables show how frequently each unique value appears in a set. A **relative frequency table** is one that shows the proportions of each unique value compared to the entire set. Relative frequencies are given as percentages; however, the total percent for a relative frequency table will not necessarily equal 100 percent due to rounding. An example of a frequency table with relative frequencies is below.

Favorite Color	Frequency	Relative Frequency
Blue	4	13%
Red	7	22%
Green	3	9%
Purple	6	19%
Cyan	12	38%

Circle Graphs

Circle graphs, also known as *pie charts*, provide a visual depiction of the relationship of each type of data compared to the whole set of data. The circle graph is divided into sections by drawing radii to create central angles whose percentage of the circle is equal to the individual data's percentage of the whole set. Each 1% of data is equal to 3.6° in the circle graph. Therefore, data represented by a 90° section of the circle graph makes up 25% of the whole. When complete, a circle graph often looks like a pie cut into uneven wedges. The pie chart below shows the data from the frequency table referenced earlier where people were asked their favorite color.

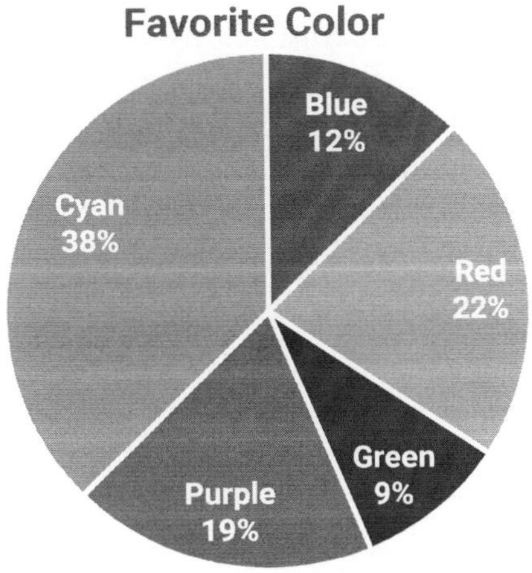

PICTOGRAPHS

A **pictograph** is a graph, generally in the horizontal orientation, that uses pictures or symbols to represent the data. Each pictograph must have a key that defines the picture or symbol and gives the quantity each picture or symbol represents. Pictures or symbols on a pictograph are not always shown as whole elements. In this case, the fraction of the picture or symbol shown represents the same fraction of the quantity a whole picture or symbol stands for. For example, a row with $3\frac{1}{2}$ ears of corn, where each ear of corn represents 100 stalks of corn in a field, would equal $3\frac{1}{2} \times 100 = 350$ stalks of corn in the field.

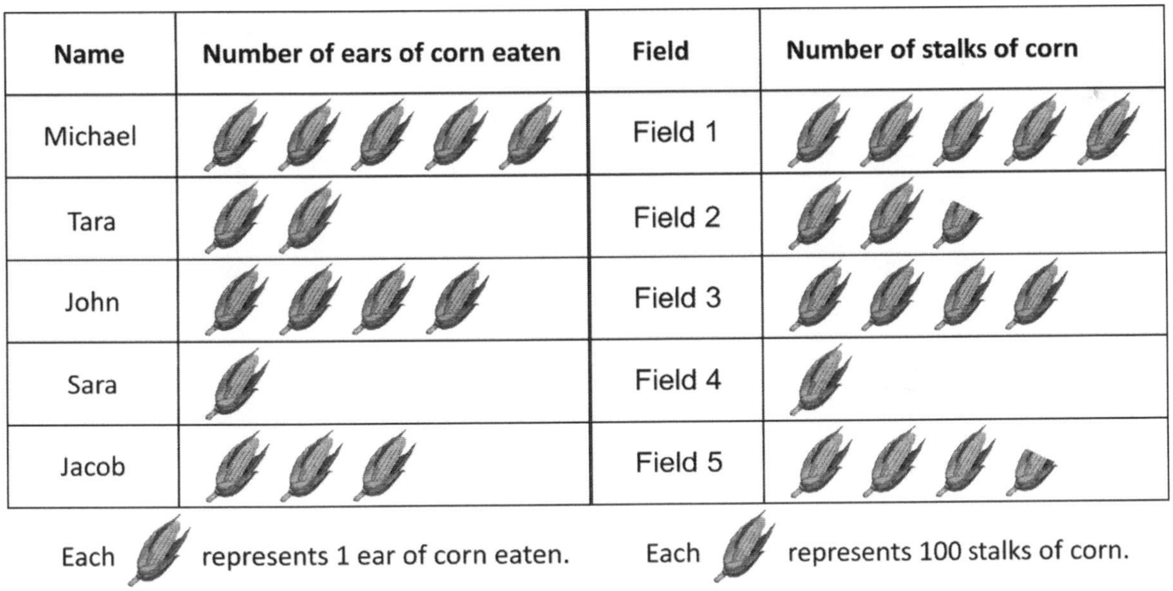

Review Video: Pictographs
Visit mometrix.com/academy and enter code: 147860

LINE GRAPHS

Line graphs have one or more lines of varying styles (solid or broken) to show the different values for a set of data. The individual data are represented as ordered pairs, much like on a Cartesian plane. In this case, the *x*- and *y*-axes are defined in terms of their units, such as dollars or time. The individual plotted points are joined by line segments to show whether the value of the data is increasing (line sloping upward), decreasing (line sloping downward), or staying the same (horizontal line). Multiple sets of data can be graphed on the same line graph to give an easy visual comparison. An example of this would be graphing achievement test scores for different groups of students over the same time period to see which group had the greatest increase or decrease in performance from year to year (as shown below).

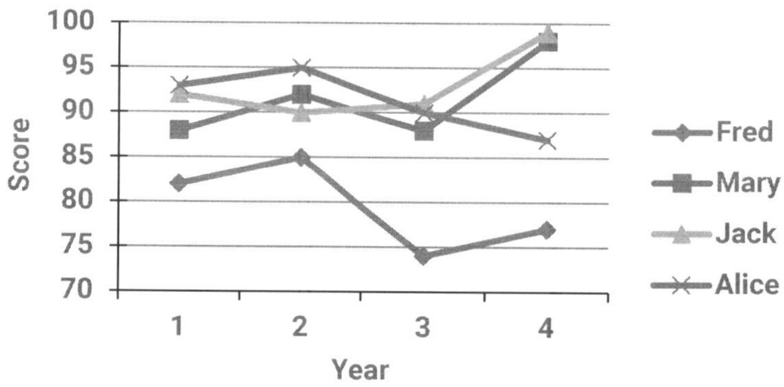

Review Video: How to Create a Line Graph
Visit mometrix.com/academy and enter code: 480147

LINE PLOTS

A **line plot**, also known as a *dot plot*, has plotted points that are not connected by line segments. In this graph, the horizontal axis lists the different possible values for the data, and the vertical axis lists the number of times the individual value occurs. A single dot is graphed for each value to show the number of times it occurs. This graph is more closely related to a bar graph than a line graph. Do not connect the dots in a line plot or it will misrepresent the data.

Review Video: Line Plot
Visit mometrix.com/academy and enter code: 754610

STEM AND LEAF PLOTS

A **stem and leaf plot** is useful for depicting groups of data that fall into a range of values. Each piece of data is separated into two parts: the first, or left, part is called the stem; the second, or right, part is called the leaf. Each stem is listed in a column from smallest to largest. Each leaf that has the common stem is listed in that stem's row from smallest to largest. For example, in a set of two-digit numbers, the digit in the tens place is the stem, and the digit in the ones place is the leaf. With a stem and leaf plot, you can easily see which subset of numbers (10s, 20s, 30s, etc.) is the largest. This information is also readily available by looking at a histogram, but a stem and leaf plot also allows you to look closer and see exactly which values fall in that range. Using a sample set of test scores (82, 88, 92, 93, 85, 90, 92, 95, 74, 88, 90, 91, 78, 87, 98, 99), we can assemble a stem and leaf plot like the one below.

Test Scores

Stem	Leaves
7	4 8
8	2 5 7 8 8
9	0 0 1 2 2 3 5 8 9

Review Video: Stem-and-Leaf Plots
Visit mometrix.com/academy and enter code: 302339

Bar Graphs

A **bar graph** is one of the few graphs that can be drawn correctly in two different configurations – both horizontally and vertically. A bar graph is similar to a line plot in the way the data is organized on the graph. Both axes must have their categories defined for the graph to be useful. Rather than placing a single dot to mark the point of the data's value, a bar, or thick line, is drawn from zero to the exact value of the data, whether it is a number, percentage, or other numerical value. Longer bar lengths correspond to greater data values. To read a bar graph, read the labels for the axes to find the units being reported. Then, look where the bars end in relation to the scale given on the corresponding axis and determine the associated value.

The bar chart below represents the responses from our favorite-color survey.

Favorite Color

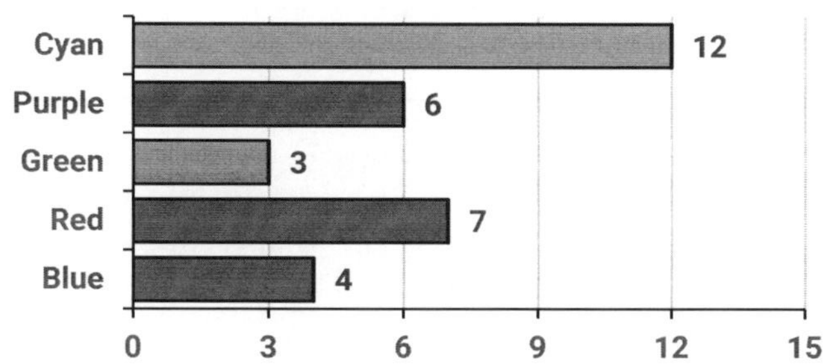

Scientific Models

Scientists often create **models** to help express and understand scientific ideas. A model is a representation of an idea that is used to experience something that cannot be experienced directly. For instance, we cannot see and experience evaporation directly, but we can easily draw out the process of evaporation, condensation, and precipitation. Having a drawing helps us to understand the concept since we cannot experience it directly. Models can be three-dimensional, such as something you can hold, or they can be simple diagrams demonstrating a process. For instance, a planetarium is a large model that helps someone see the size of planets and stars and how they interact. More typical models in the classroom include baking soda and vinegar volcanoes, solar system mobiles, or molecules made from foam and straws. Other models can include a diagram showing the water cycle.

Limitations of Models

Using models can be very helpful for experiencing a scientific process that normally couldn't be observed directly, but they are naturally limited. Models are usually used to express a very large thing in a small way, such as a volcano or the planet Earth in a way that a human can look at it and touch it. Models are also often used to express very small things or invisible things in a more observable way. Changing the size or the materials used to express something heavily limits how effective a model is. For instance, if a model on the water cycle used cotton balls to show clouds, it impairs our understanding of clouds. Clouds are not made of dry, solid cotton, but are made up of vapor filled with water. Volcanos made from clay and that use baking soda and vinegar do not demonstrate the extreme heat or mass of volcanic materials. Similarly, a mobile of the solar system cannot express how extremely large the Sun and planets are. When using a model to understand a concept, the observer needs to be aware that they are probably only getting a clear picture of one side of the concept, and not understanding it fully.

Tools for Measuring and Observation

Purpose	Tool
Measuring Length	Rulers, meter sticks
Measuring Weight or Mass	Spring scales, pan balances
Measuring Volume	Beakers, graduated cylinders
Measuring Time	Timers, clocks
Measuring Temperature	Thermometer
Recording Information	Journals, notebooks
Observing Animals and Plants	Terrariums, aquariums, collecting nets
Observing Weather	Rain Gauges, wind vanes,
Models for Understanding Concepts	Sun-Earth-Moon System Models, volcano models, water cycle models
Visual Observation	cameras, hand lenses, microscopes

Science Careers

Almost all fields require people who think like scientists or use science directly.

- **Meteorologists** – study the atmosphere to predict weather.
- **Engineers** – use physics and chemistry to design complicated technology and processes.
- **Doctors** – use biology to learn how the body and disease works.
- **Astronomers** – use physics and space science to study the Earth and the universe and travel into space.

Contributions of Scientists

- **Sir Francis Bacon** – contributed many ideas that helped develop the modern scientific method.
- **Gallileo Galilei**– one of the first people to use a telescope and contributed ideas about how gravity works. He also contributed the idea that the Earth revolved around the Sun, and not the other way around.
- **Leonardo da Vinci** – known for his contributions to art and to science, he was an avid inventor, designing a submarine, an armored tank, and several aircraft far before any of which were actually built.
- **Sir Isaac Newton** – best known for his contributions to physics. He described the principals of inertia and friction.
- **Louis Pasteur** – discovered bacteria and invented the process of pasteurization and developed some of the first vaccines.

- **Thomas Edison** – invented many distinct devices, including the phonograph, improved upon the telephone, the lightbulb, and the kinetoscope, an early form of movie projector.
- **Albert Einstein** – studied theoretical physics with the use of mathematics and is particularly famous for his theory of relativity

Matter and Energy

Atomic Models and Theories

There have been many theories regarding the **structure** of atoms and their particles. Part of the challenge in developing an understanding of matter is that atoms and their particles are too small to be seen. It is believed that the first conceptualization of the atom was developed by **Democritus** in 400 B.C. Some of the more notable models are the solid sphere or billiard ball model postulated by **John Dalton**, the plum pudding or raisin bun model by **J.J. Thomson**, the planetary or nuclear model by **Ernest Rutherford**, the Bohr or orbit model by **Niels Bohr**, and the electron cloud or quantum mechanical model by **Louis de Broglie** and **Erwin Schrodinger**. Rutherford directed the alpha scattering experiment that discounted the plum pudding model. The shortcoming of the Bohr model was the belief that electrons orbited in fixed rather than changing ecliptic orbits.

Review Video: Atomic Models
Visit mometrix.com/academy and enter code: 434851

Review Video: John Dalton
Visit mometrix.com/academy and enter code: 565627

Thomson "Plum Pudding" Model

J.J. Thomson, the discoverer of the electron, suggested that the arrangement of protons and electrons within an atom could be approximated by dried fruit in a **plum pudding**. Thomson, whose discovery of the electron preceded that of the proton or neutron, hypothesized that an atom's electrons, the dried plums, were positioned uniformly inside the atom within a cloud of positive charge, the pudding. This model was later disproved.

Rutherford Scattering

Ernest Rutherford concluded from the work of Geiger and Marsden that the majority of the mass was concentrated in a minute, positively charged region, the **nucleus**, which was surrounded by **electrons**. When a positive alpha particle approached close enough to the nucleus, it was strongly repelled, enough so that it had the ability to rebound at high angles. The small nucleus size explained the small number of alpha particles that were repelled in this fashion. The scattering led to development of the **planetary model of the atom**, which was further developed by Niels Bohr into what is now known as the Bohr model.

Bohr Model

Niels Bohr postulated that the electrons orbiting the nucleus must occupy discrete orbits. These discrete orbits also corresponded to discrete levels of energy and angular momentum. Consequently, the only way that electrons could move between orbits was by making nearly instantaneous jumps between them. These jumps, known as **quantum leaps**, are associated with the absorption or emission of a quantum of energy, known as a photon. If the electron is jumping to a higher energy state, a photon must be absorbed. Similarly, if the electron is dropping to a lower energy state, a photon must be emitted.

Review Video: Structure of Atoms
Visit mometrix.com/academy and enter code: 905932

Basic Organization of Matter

An **element** is the most basic type of matter. It has unique properties and cannot be broken down into other elements. The smallest unit of an element is the **atom**. A chemical combination of two or more types of elements is called a compound. **Compounds** often have properties that are very different from those of their constituent elements. The smallest independent unit of an element or compound is known as a **molecule**. Most elements are found somewhere in nature in single-atom form, but a few elements only exist naturally in pairs. These are called diatomic elements, of which some of the most common are hydrogen, nitrogen, and oxygen. Elements and compounds are represented by chemical symbols, one or two letters, most often the first in the element name. More than one atom of the same element in a compound is represented with a subscript number designating how many atoms of that element are present. Water, for instance, contains two hydrogens and one oxygen. Thus, the chemical formula is H_2O. Methane contains one carbon and four hydrogens, so its formula is CH_4.

Review Video: Molecules
Visit mometrix.com/academy and enter code: 349910

Atom

A **neutral atom** consists of an extremely dense **nucleus** composed of one or more positively-charged **protons** and a varying number of uncharged **neutrons**, except for hydrogen-1 which contains no neutrons, surrounded by a cloud of one or more negatively-charged **electrons**. In a neutral atom, the number of electrons equals the number of protons in the nucleus. The protons and neutrons are bound together by the strong nuclear force, which overcomes the repulsive force the positive charges of the protons have for each other. The negatively-charged electrons are bound to the positively-charged protons by the attractive electromagnetic force. The number of protons, or the atomic number, determines the chemical element the atom represents. The number of electrons in the outermost shell determines how the atom interacts with other atoms or molecules.

Protons, Neutrons, and Electrons

The three major subatomic particles are the proton, neutron, and electron. The **proton**, which is located in the nucleus, has a relative charge of +1. The **neutron**, which is located in the nucleus, has a relative charge of 0. The **electron**, which is located outside the nucleus, has a relative charge of −1. The proton and neutron, which are essentially the same mass, are much more massive than the electron and make up the mass of the atom. The electron's mass is insignificant compared to the mass of the proton and neutron.

Atomic Number and Mass Number

The **atomic number** of an element is the number of protons in the nucleus of an atom of that element. This is the number that identifies the type of an atom. For example, all oxygen atoms have eight protons, and all carbon atoms have six protons. Each element is identified by its specific atomic number.

The **mass number** is the number of protons and neutrons in the nucleus of an atom. Although the atomic number is the same for all atoms of a specific element, the mass number can vary due to the varying numbers of neutrons in various isotopes of the atom.

Periodic Table

The **periodic table** groups elements with similar chemical properties together. The grouping of elements is based on atomic structure. It shows periodic trends of physical and chemical properties and identifies families of elements with similar properties. It is a common model for organizing and understanding elements. In the periodic table, each element has its own cell that includes varying amounts of information presented in symbol form about the properties of the element. Cells in the table are arranged in rows (periods) and columns (groups or families). At minimum, a cell includes the symbol for the element and its atomic number. The cell for hydrogen, for example, which appears first in the upper left corner, includes an "H" and a "1" above the letter. Elements are ordered by atomic number, left to right, top to bottom.

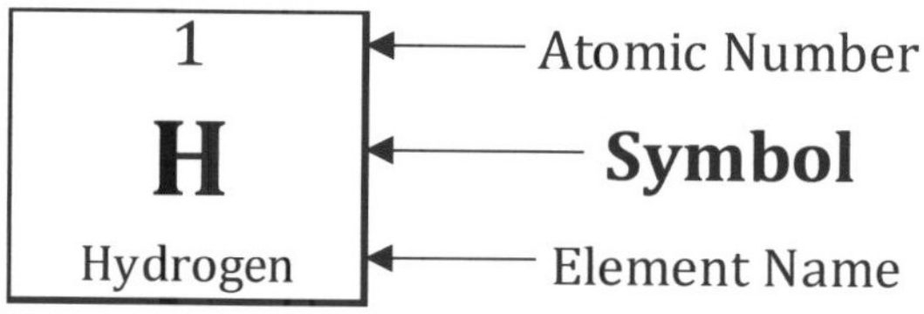

Review Video: The Periodic Table
Visit mometrix.com/academy and enter code: 154828

In the periodic table, the groups are the columns numbered 1 through 18 that group elements with similar outer electron shell configurations. Since the configuration of the outer electron shell is one of the primary factors affecting an element's chemical properties, elements within the same group have similar chemical properties. Previous naming conventions for groups have included the use of Roman numerals and upper-case letters. Currently, the periodic table groups are: Group 1, alkali metals; Group 2, alkaline earth metals; Groups 3-12, transition metals; Group 13, boron family; Group 14; carbon family; Group 15, pnictogens; Group 16, chalcogens; Group 17, halogens; Group 18, noble gases.

In the periodic table, there are seven periods (rows), and within each period there are blocks that group elements with the same outer electron subshell (more on this in the next section). The number of electrons in that outer shell determines which group an element belongs to within a given block. Each row's number (1, 2, 3, etc.) corresponds to the highest number electron shell that is in use. For example, row 2 uses only electron shells 1 and 2, while row 7 uses all shells from 1-7.

Groups and Periods in the Periodic Table

A **group** is a vertical column of the periodic table. Elements in the same group have the same number of **valence electrons**. For the representative elements, the number of valence electrons is equal to the group number. Because of their equal valence electrons, elements in the same groups have similar physical and chemical properties. A period is a horizontal row of the periodic table. Atomic number increases from left to right across a row. The **period** of an element corresponds to the **highest energy level** of the electrons in the atoms of that element. The energy level increases from top to bottom down a group.

Period ↓ / Group →	1	2	3	4	5	6	7	8	9	10	11	12	13	14	15	16	17	18
1	1 H																	2 He
2	3 Li	4 Be											5 B	6 C	7 N	8 O	9 F	10 Ne
3	11 Na	12 Mg											13 Al	14 Si	15 P	16 S	17 Cl	18 Ar
4	19 K	20 Ca	21 Sc	22 Ti	23 V	24 Cr	25 Mn	26 Fe	27 Co	28 Ni	29 Cu	30 Zn	31 Ga	32 Ge	33 As	34 Se	35 Br	36 Kr
5	37 Rb	38 Sr	39 Y	40 Zr	41 Nb	42 Mo	43 Tc	44 Ru	45 Rh	46 Pd	47 Ag	48 Cd	49 In	50 Sn	51 Sb	52 Te	53 I	54 Xe
6	55 Cs	56 Ba	*	72 Hf	73 Ta	74 W	75 Re	76 Os	77 Ir	78 Pt	79 Au	80 Hg	81 Tl	82 Pb	83 Bi	84 Po	85 At	86 Rn
7	87 Fr	88 Ra	**	104 Rf	105 Db	106 Sg	107 Bh	108 Hs	109 Mt	110 Ds	111 Rg	112 Cn	113 Uut	114 Fl	115 Uup	116 Lv	117 Uus	118 Uuo

*	57 La	58 Ce	59 Pr	60 Nd	61 Pm	62 Sm	63 Eu	64 Gd	65 Tb	66 Dy	67 Ho	68 Er	69 Tm	70 Yb	71 Lu
**	89 Ac	90 Th	91 Pa	92 U	93 Np	94 Pu	95 Am	96 Cm	97 Bk	98 Cf	99 Es	100 Fm	101 Md	102 No	103 Lr

Atomic Number and Atomic Mass in the Periodic Table

The elements in the periodic table are arranged in order of **increasing atomic number** first left to right and then top to bottom across the periodic table. The **atomic number** represents the number of protons in the atoms of that element. Because of the increasing numbers of protons, the atomic mass typically also increases from left to right across a period and from top to bottom down a row. The **atomic mass** is a weighted average of all the naturally occurring isotopes of an element.

Atomic Symbols

The **atomic symbol** for many elements is simply the first letter of the element name. For example, the atomic symbol for hydrogen is H, and the atomic symbol for carbon is C. The atomic symbol of other elements is the first two letters of the element name. For example, the atomic symbol for helium is He, and the atomic symbol for cobalt is Co. The atomic symbols of several elements are derived from Latin. For example, the atomic symbol for copper (Cu) is derived from *cuprum,* and the atomic symbol for iron (Fe) is derived from *ferrum.* The atomic symbol for tungsten (W) is derived from the German word *wolfram*.

Arrangement of Metals, Nonmetals, and Metalloids in the Periodic Table

The **metals** are located on the left side and center of the periodic table, and the **nonmetals** are located on the right side of the periodic table. The **metalloids** or **semimetals** form a zigzag line between the metals and nonmetals as shown below. Metals include the alkali metals such as lithium, sodium, and potassium and the alkaline earth metals such as beryllium, magnesium, and calcium. Metals also include the transition metals such as iron, copper, and nickel and the inner transition metals such as thorium, uranium, and plutonium. Nonmetals include the chalcogens such as oxygen and sulfur, the halogens such as fluorine and chlorine, and the noble gases such as helium and argon. Carbon, nitrogen, and phosphorus are also nonmetals. Metalloids or semimetals include boron, silicon, germanium, antimony, and polonium.

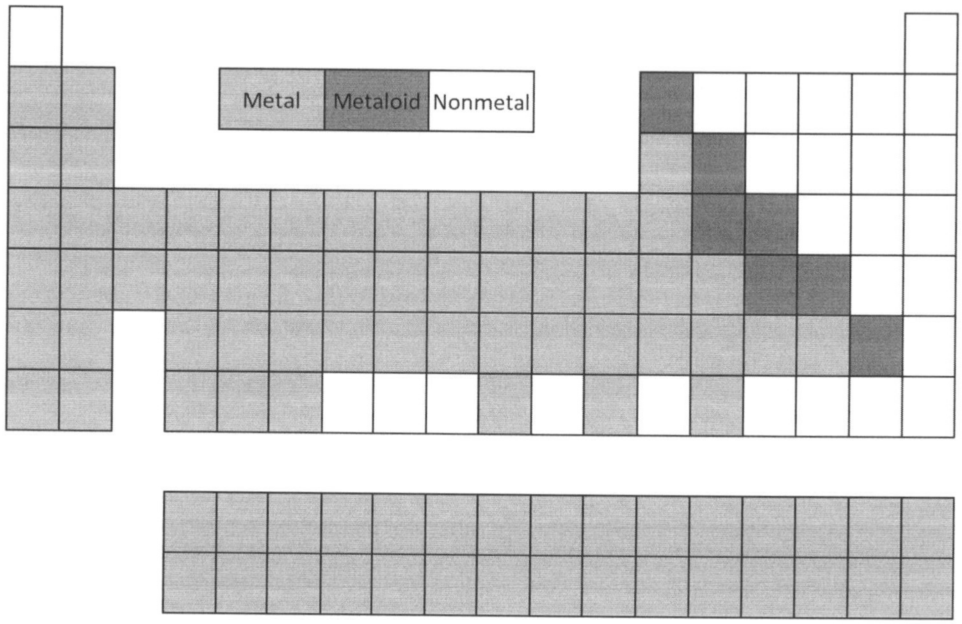

Arrangement of Transition Elements

The **transition elements** belong to one of two categories—transition metals or inner transition metals. The **transition metals** are located in the middle of the periodic table, and the inner transition metals are typically set off as two rows by themselves at the bottom of the periodic table. The transition metals correspond to the "*d* block" for orbital filling, and the inner transition metals correspond to the "*f* block" for orbital filling. Examples of transition metals include iron, copper, nickel, and zinc. The inner transition metals consist of the *lanthanide* or *rare-earth series*, which corresponds to the first row, and the *actinide series*, which corresponds to the second row of the inner transition metals. The *lanthanide series* includes lanthanum, cerium, and praseodymium. The *actinide series* includes actinium, uranium, and plutonium.

Periodic Trends

Atomic Radius Size

Atomic radius size decreases across a period from left to right and increases down a group from top to bottom. The atomic radius decreases across a period due to the increasing number of protons and the attraction between those protons and the orbiting electrons. The atomic radius increases down a group due to the increasing energy levels. Atoms in the top-right corner of the periodic table (including hydrogen) have the smallest atomic radii, and atoms in the bottom-left corner of the periodic table have the largest atomic radii. Helium has the smallest atomic radius, and cesium has the largest confirmed atomic radius.

Ionic Radius Size

The **ionic radius size** increases down a group of the periodic table. This is due to the increasing energy levels and the fact that electrons are orbiting farther and farther from the nucleus. The trend seen across the periods of the periodic table is due to the formation of cations or anions. Metals form cations or positive ions. Cations are smaller than their neutral atoms due to the loss of one or more electrons. Nonmetals except the noble gases form anions or negative ions. Anions are larger than their neutral atoms due to the gain of one or more electrons.

Ionization Energy

Ionization energy is the amount of energy needed to remove an electron from an isolated atom. Ionization energy decreases down a group of the periodic table because the electrons get farther and farther from the nucleus making it easier for the electron to be removed. Ionization energy increases across a period of the periodic table due to the decreasing atomic size, which is due to the increasing number of protons attracting the electrons towards the nucleus. These trends of ionization energy are the opposite of the trends for atomic radius.

Electron Affinity

Electron affinity is the energy required to add an electron to a neutral atom in the gaseous phase of an element. If electrons are added to a halogen such as fluorine or chlorine, energy is released and the electron affinity is negative. If electrons are added to an alkaline earth metal, energy is absorbed and the electron affinity is positive. In general, electron affinity becomes more negative from left to right across a period in the periodic table. Electron affinity becomes less negative from the top to the bottom of a group of the periodic table.

Electronegativity

Electronegativity is a measure of the ability of an atom that is chemically combined to at least one other atom in a molecule to attract electrons to it. The Pauling scale is commonly used to assign values to the elements, with fluorine, which is the most electronegative element, being assigned a value of 4.0. Electronegativity increases from left to right across a period of the periodic table and decreases from top to bottom down a group of the periodic table.

Review Video: Electron Configuration
Visit mometrix.com/academy and enter code: 565113

Review Video: Electronegativity
Visit mometrix.com/academy and enter code: 823348

Physical Properties of the Elements in Relation to the Periodic Table

The **boiling point**, **melting point**, and **conductivity** of the elements depend partially on the number of valence electrons of the atoms of those elements. For the representative elements in groups 1A–8A, the number of valence electrons matches the group number. Because all of the elements in each individual group contain the same number of valence electrons, elements in the same groups tend to have similar boiling points, melting points, and conductivity. Boiling points and melting points tend to decrease moving down the column of groups 1A–4A and 8A but increase slightly moving down the column of groups 5A–7A.

Chemical Reactivity in Relation to the Periodic Table

Atoms of elements in the same **group** or **family** of the periodic table tend to have **similar chemical properties** and **similar chemical reactions**. For example, the alkali metals, which form cations with a charge of +1, tend to react with water to form hydrogen gas and metal hydroxides. The alkaline earth metals, which form cations with a charge of +2, react with oxygen gas to form metal oxides. The halogens, which form anions with a charge of –1, are highly reactive and toxic. The noble gases are unreactive and never form compounds naturally.

Chemical Formulas

A chemical formula is a set of letters, numbers, and symbols that describe the elemental composition of a particular substance. Elements are listed by their periodic table symbol. A subscript number after the element symbol indicates the number of that type of element's atoms in the formula. If there is no subscript, there is only one atom of that type of element. There are three common types of chemical formulas to be familiar with:

1. The *molecular formula* describes the elemental composition of a single molecule of a substance. For instance, the molecular formula for glucose is $C_6H_{12}O_6$, because each molecule of glucose contains six atoms of carbon and oxygen, and twelve atoms of hydrogen.

2. The *empirical formula* is a reduced form of the molecular formula that gives only the ratios of the elements in a substance. For instance, the empirical formula for glucose is CH_2O, because the ratio of carbon to hydrogen to oxygen in glucose is 1 to 2 to 1. The empirical formula will be the same as the molecular formula for many simple substances.

3. The *structural formula* is an expanded formula that gives information about the way that the atoms in a molecule are bonded. Below is an example of the structural formula for ethane:

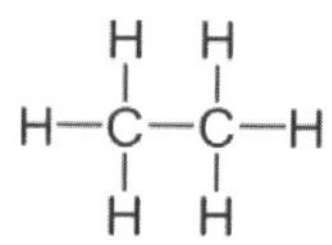

CHEMICAL EQUATION

Chemical equations describe chemical reactions. The reactants are on the left side before the arrow. The products are on the right side after the arrow. The arrow is the mark that points to the reaction or change. The coefficient is the number before the element. This gives the ratio of reactants to products in terms of moles.

The equation for making water from hydrogen and oxygen is $2H_{2(g)} + O_{2(g)} \rightarrow 2H_2O_{(l)}$. The number 2 before hydrogen and water is the coefficient. This means that there are 2 moles of hydrogen and 2 of water. There is 1 mole of oxygen. This does not need to have the number 1 before the symbol for the element. For additional information, the following subscripts are often included to indicate the state of the substance: (g) stands for gas, (l) stands for liquid, (s) stands for solid, and (aq) stands for aqueous. Aqueous means the substance is dissolved in water. Charges are shown by superscript for individual ions, not for ionic compounds. Polyatomic ions are separated by parentheses. This is done so the kind of ion will not be confused with the number of ions.

Review Video: The Process of a Reaction
Visit mometrix.com/academy and enter code: 808039

In a chemical equation, it is necessary to have the same number of atoms for each element on each side of the equation. Reactants appear on the left side of the equation and the products appear on the right. The elements are balanced by placing the necessary coefficients in front of each element or compound. In a simple example, diatomic hydrogen (H_2) combines with diatomic oxygen (O_2) to form water:

$$H_2 + O_2 \rightarrow H_2O$$

Adding up all the atoms for each element shows that there is one more oxygen on the reactant side than the product side of the equation. Since water contains twice as many hydrogen atoms as oxygen atoms, placing the coefficient 2 in front of both the hydrogen molecule on the reactant side and the water molecule on the product side balances the equation:

$$2\ H_2 + O_2 \rightarrow 2\ H_2O$$

Again, count the number of atoms of each element on both sides of the equation. There are 4 hydrogen atoms and 2 oxygen atoms on each side of the equation so it is balanced.

Review Video: Balancing Chemical Equations
Visit mometrix.com/academy and enter code: 341228

Chemical and Physical Changes

Physical changes do not produce new substances. The atoms or molecules may be rearranged, but no new substances are formed. **Phase changes** or changes of state such as melting, freezing, and sublimation are physical changes. For example, physical changes include the melting of ice, the boiling of water, sugar dissolving into water, and the crushing of a piece of chalk into a fine powder.

Chemical changes involve a **chemical reaction** and do produce new substances. When iron rusts, iron oxide is formed, indicating a chemical change. Other examples of chemical changes include baking a cake, burning wood, digesting food, and mixing an acid and a base.

Law of Conservation of Energy

The **law of conservation of energy** states that in a closed system, energy cannot be created or destroyed but only changed from one form to another. This is also known as the first law of thermodynamics. Another way to state this is that the **total energy in an isolated system is constant**. Energy comes in many forms that may be transformed from one kind to another, but in a closed system, the total amount of energy is conserved or remains constant. For example, potential energy can be converted to kinetic energy, thermal energy, radiant energy, or mechanical energy. In an isolated chemical reaction, there can be no energy created or destroyed. The energy simply changes forms.

Law of Conservation of Mass

The **law of conservation of mass** is also known as the **law of conservation of matter**. This basically means that in a closed system, the total mass of the products must equal the total mass of the reactants. This could also be stated that in a closed system, mass never changes. A consequence of this law is that matter is never created or destroyed during a typical chemical reaction. The atoms of the reactants are simply rearranged to form the products. The number and type of each specific atom involved in the reactants is identical to the number and type of atoms in the products. This is the key principle used when balancing chemical equations. In a balanced chemical equation, the number of moles of each element on the reactant side equals the number of moles of each element on the product side.

Conversion of Energy Within Chemical Systems

Chemical energy is the energy stored in molecules in the bonds between the atoms of those molecules and the energy associated with the intermolecular forces. This stored **potential energy** may be converted into **kinetic energy** and then into heat. During a chemical reaction, atoms may be rearranged and chemical bonds may be formed or broken accompanied by a corresponding absorption or release of energy, usually in the form of heat. According to the first law of thermodynamics, during these energy conversions, the **total amount of energy must be conserved**.

Intensive and Extensive Physical Properties of Matter

Intensive properties are those that do not depend upon the size of the sample. Examples are density, melting-freezing point, boiling point, color, chemical reactivity, luster, malleability, and electrical conductivity. **Extensive properties** do depend on the size of the sample. Examples include the amount of space occupied (volume), mass, and weight. Note that mass and weight are not the same thing. Mass is the amount of material present in a body, whereas weight is the gravitational force acting upon that mass in a specific gravitational field. A 100-kilogram object has the same mass on Earth as on the Moon, but its weight will change markedly. It will weigh 980.7 Newtons (220.5 pounds) here on Earth, but only 163.5 N (36.75 lbs) on the Moon. In outer space this object would weigh nothing at all, but would still have a mass of 100 kg.

Properties of Matter

Matter is anything that takes up space and has weight. Even air has weight and takes up space. All types of matter have different properties that can be observed or measured. There are many properties of matter, including temperature, mass, magnetism, and the ability to sink or float.

Temperature

Temperature is a property that tells how hot or cold a thing is. **Temperature** also demonstrates how much **thermal energy** is in a thing. When an object is cold, it has very little thermal energy. For many substances, being hot makes the substance expand, while being cold makes it shrink. Temperature also tends to transfer from one object to another. For instance, when a cup is filled with ice and water, the ice and water exchange energy until they are the same temperature. The ice and water reach the same temperature eventually, usually resulting in the ice melting.

Mass and Weight

Mass is a measure of how much **matter** is in an object. **Mass** is usually measured by placing an object on a scale. The terms mass and weight are often used interchangeably, but they actually have different definitions. Mass is always the same for a specific object, but **weight** depends on other factors. For instance, 1,000 lb. car always has the same mass, but it would weigh different amounts depending on if the car were on Earth or on Mars, which has much lower gravity.

Volume and Density

Volume is a measure of the **size** of an object or how much space an object takes up. Volume affects several other factors like density. Density is the amount of **mass** (amount of matter) in a certain **volume**. The more matter there is, the more mass an object has. **Density** takes into account both the mass and volume of an object. For instance, an inflated balloon has very little mass in it, but it is fairly large. A watermelon is about the same size, but has much more mass in it, so the watermelon is denser than the balloon. Density is the reason things float or sink. One example is oil and water. Oil is usually thicker than water, but it is actually less dense. If you put oil and water in a cup, you can see that the oil always **floats** to the top. Another way of thinking about it is that the water is actually **sinking** in the oil.

Calculating Density

As stated before, density is the amount of mass in a certain volume. The formula used to find an object's density is $\text{Density} = \frac{\text{Mass}}{\text{Volume}}$. The formula is the same for liquid measurements of volume. Since volume is a measurement of the ratio of mass to volume, both units are required in the final answer.

For example, if a cube has a mass of 50 grams and the volume of 64 cm^3, the mass of 50 grams is divided by 64 to find that the density is 0.5 grams/cm^3.

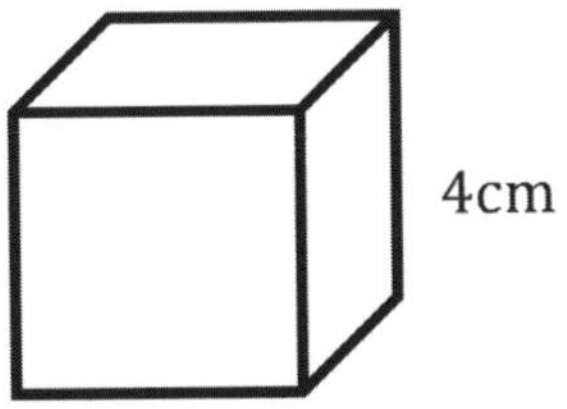

Mass = 50 grams

$$\text{Volume} = \text{side} \times \text{side} \times \text{side}$$
$$64 = 4 \times 4 \times 4$$
$$\text{Density} = \frac{\text{Mass}}{\text{Volume}}$$
$$D = \frac{50\text{g}}{64\text{cm}^3}$$
$$\text{Density} = 0.78 \text{ grams per cm}^3$$

Density of Water

Density is the **mass** (amount of matter) in a certain **volume**. The more **matter** there is, the more the object weighs. Most solids have more matter than the same volume of their liquids. This means that they are denser and sink in their own liquid. However, water is different. The molecules in ice are farther apart than they are in liquid water. That means that ice has less matter in it than the same volume of liquid water. Therefore, ice is less dense and floats in water.

Materials Denser Than Water

Ships and other floating objects made of materials that are denser than water float because of the empty space they contain inside their hulls. A ship weighing 5,000 tons overall will displace 5,000 tons of water, but this weight of water will occupy a smaller volume than the ship itself. Once this amount of water has been displaced the ship will not sink any deeper into the water and will float. Archimedes' principle states that the buoyant force is equal to the weight of the water (or any other fluid displaced). The reason a solid piece of iron or a rock sinks is that it weighs more than the volume of water it displaces. For the same reason, because a helium-filled balloon is lighter than air it will rise until the air's density is reduced such that the volume of air displaced is the same as the volume of the balloon.

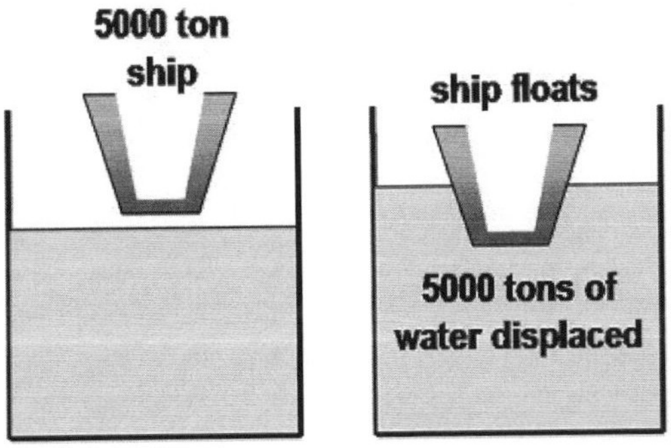

Density of Water and Ice

Most solids have more matter than the same volume of their liquids. This means that they are denser and sink in their own liquid. However, water is different. The molecules in ice are farther apart than they are in liquid water. That means that ice has less matter in it than the same volume of liquid water. Therefore, ice is less dense and floats in water.

Magnetism

Magnetism is a property that some rocks or metals can possess. **Magnetism** is a force that can push or pull on other magnetic materials. Magnets always have two poles, which attract the opposite pole and repel the same pole. Usually, the poles on a magnet are identified as being North or South, because the Earth's North and South Poles are actually magnetic as well. This is the reason that compasses work. The small needle in a compass is attracted to the Earth's poles and points in that direction. Many types of technology use magnetism, including electronics, motors, credit cards, and others.

Magnets

A magnet is a metal or object that produces a magnetic field. A magnetic field is mapped by invisible curved lines of force that attract magnets or certain metals like iron or nickel. A simple bar magnet has a south pole (S) at one end and a north pole (N) at the other. Each pole will attract the opposite pole of another magnet and repel the same pole. The north pole of a compass needle will point to the south pole of a magnet, while the south pole of the needle will be attracted to the north pole of the magnet.

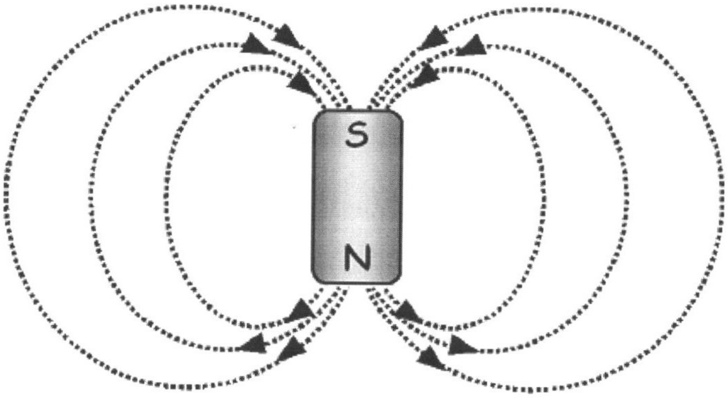

Opposite Poles of Two Magnets Attract Each Other

When two bar magnets are lined end to end with the north and south poles near each other, the lines of force run from the north pole of one magnet to the south pole of the other magnet indicating attraction.

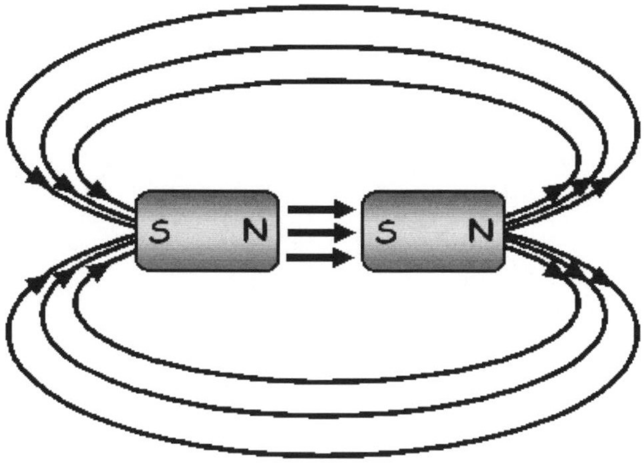

Cutting a Bar Magnet in Two

If a bar magnet is cut in two, two complete magnets will form, each with a north and south pole. If a bar magnet is cut it into three parts, three magnets will form.

Poles of Two Magnets Repel Each Other

When the like poles of two magnets are brought close to each other the lines of force run in opposite directions. This causes the two poles to push each other away.

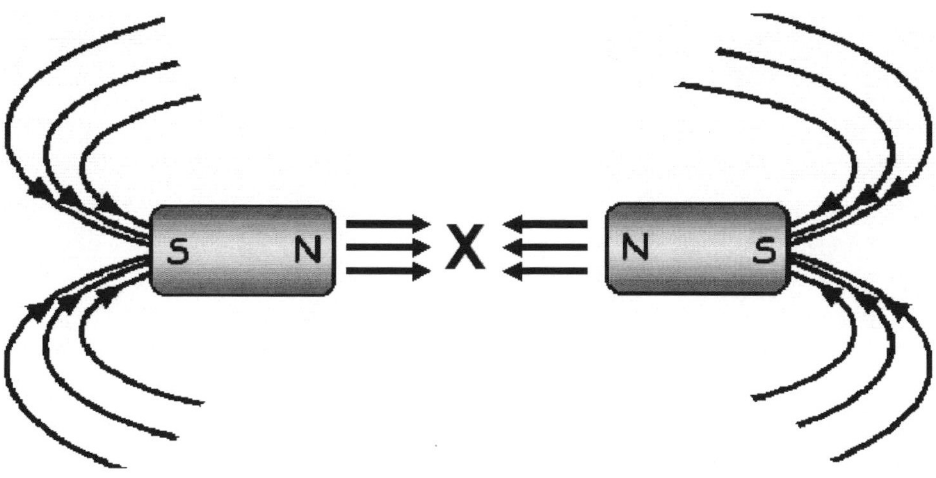

Needle of a Magnetic Compass

Planet Earth has a magnetic field just like a bar magnet. The north pole of a compass needle points to Earth's north pole because the magnetic pole near the North Pole is actually the south pole of Earth's magnetic field. Likewise, the south pole of the compass needle is attracted to the north pole of Earth's magnetic field near the south geographic pole. Just remember that each magnetic pole is attracted to its opposite pole on another magnet or magnetic object.

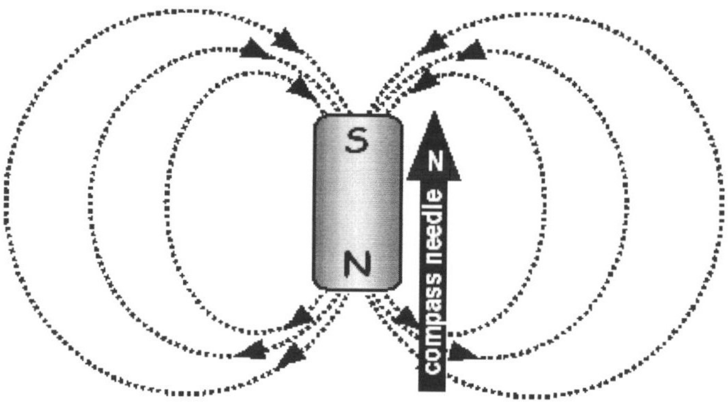

Conductivity

Conductivity is a property that describes how easily a material **transfers energy** to and from other materials. **Conductivity** usually refers to either heat energy or electrical energy. For instance, metals are usually good at conducting both heat and electricity, whereas plastic usually is not good at conducting these types of energy. Materials that are good at transferring energy are known as **conductors**, whereas materials that are not good at transferring energy are known as **resistors**.

Physical Changes

Physical changes are those that do not affect the chemical properties of a substance. Changes in state are **physical changes**. For example, a liquid can freeze into a solid or boil into a gas without changing the chemical nature of the substance. It is all still the same substance. Ice, steam, and liquid water are all still water, H_2O. Physical properties include such features as shape, texture, size, volume, mass, and density. Cutting, melting, dissolving, mixing, breaking, and crushing are all types of physical changes.

Chemical Changes

Chemical changes occur when chemical bonds are broken and new ones are formed. The original substances are **transformed** into different substances. If vinegar and baking soda are mixed together, a lot of bubbles (carbon dioxide) and water will form. Burning wood in a fireplace is another type of chemical change. The carbon in the wood reacts with oxygen in the air to make ash, carbon dioxide, smoke and energy that we feel as heat and see as light.

Examples of chemical changes include the following:

- (a) The temperature of a system changes without any heating or cooling.
- (b) The formation of a gas (bubbles).
- (c) The formation of a precipitate (solid) when two liquids are mixed.
- (d) A liquid changes color.

A **chemical change** occurs when two or more substances come together and interact in such a way that they become completely new substances. For example, two hydrogen atoms and one oxygen atom combine to make a new compound—a water molecule, H_2O. Likewise, two oxygen atoms and one carbon atom combine to make one molecule of carbon dioxide—CO_2. The two substances that combine are called **reactants,** and the new compound that emerges is the **product**. Chemical reactions (changes) can be much more complicated than this.

States of Matter

The four states of matter are solid, liquid, gas, and plasma. **Solids** have a definite shape and a definite volume. Because solid particles are held in fairly rigid positions, solids are the least compressible of the four states of matter. **Liquids** have definite volumes but no definite shapes. Because their particles are free to slip and slide over each other, liquids take the shape of their containers, but they still remain fairly incompressible by natural means. **Gases** have no definite shape or volume. Because gas particles are free to move, they move away from each other to fill their containers. Gases are compressible. **Plasmas** are high-temperature, ionized gases that exist only under very high temperatures at which electrons are stripped away from their atoms.

Review Video: States of Matter
Visit mometrix.com/academy and enter code: 742449

Review Video: Properties of Liquids
Visit mometrix.com/academy and enter code: 802024

The following table shows similarities and differences between solids, liquids, and gases:

	Solid	Liquid	Gas
Shape	Fixed shape	No fixed shape (assumes shape of container)	No fixed shape (assumes shape of container)
Volume	Fixed	Fixed	Changes to assume shape of container
Fluidity	Does not flow easily	Flows easily	Flows easily
Compressibility	Hard to compress	Hard to compress	Compresses

Six Different Types of Phase Change

A substance that is undergoing a change from a solid to a liquid is said to be melting. If this change occurs in the opposite direction, from liquid to solid, this change is called freezing. A liquid which is being converted to a gas is undergoing vaporization. The reverse of this process is known as condensation. Direct transitions from gas to solid and solid to gas are much less common in everyday life, but they can occur given the proper conditions. Solid to gas conversion is known as sublimation, while the reverse is called deposition.

Review Video: Chemical and Physical Properties of Matter
Visit mometrix.com/academy and enter code: 717349

States of Matter

The three states of matter are *solids, liquids,* and *gases.* In a **solid** the *atoms* or *molecules* of a substance are close together and locked into place. A solid has a definite shape and volume. In a liquid the atoms or molecules are farther apart. A **liquid** flows and takes the shape of its container. In a **gas** the atoms or molecules are very far apart and have a lot of energy. They will fly completely way if not held inside a container like a balloon or a closed bottle. The state of matter that a substance takes on depends mainly on temperature and pressure. For instance, candle wax is usually a solid in normal temperatures on Earth, but if it heats up, it easily melts. Paper, on the other hand, does not melt, but burns and turns directly into a gas.

Review Video: States of Matter [Advanced]
Visit mometrix.com/academy and enter code: 298130

Solid	Liquid	Gas
Have a definite shape and size. Usually denser than liquids and gases of the same material.	Have a definite size, but do not have a definite shape.	Does not have a definite size or shape, but matches its container.
• Rocks • Ice Cream • Pencils • Apples	• Milk • Water • Juice • Rain	• Steam • Fire • Helium • Fog

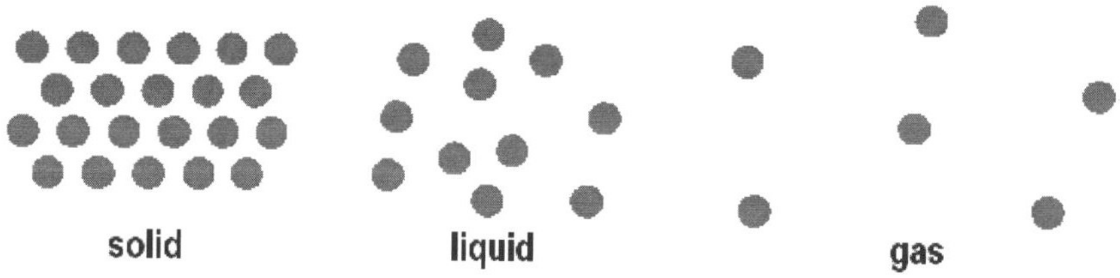

Phase States of Water

Water has three states of matter: ice, liquid water, and water vapor. Water freezes at 32 degrees Fahrenheit, where ice crystals form and the substance becomes a solid.

- **Ice** - Water crystalizes when it freezes, which means that it actually expands when it freezes, making it less dense than liquid water. This is uncommon because solids are usually the most dense form of a substance because the atoms are more tightly compressed. That is why ice actually floats in liquid water, rather than sinks.
- **Water Vapor** – Water exists in gas form as it evaporates or boils. Water vapor exists in the air and is often referred to as humidity. There is always some moisture in the air, though as the temperatures drop or pressure changes, it will condense and become liquid water again. Just like all other gas forms, water vapor spreads out in its container and flows much like a liquid.
- **Liquid Water** – Liquid water is the most common form on Earth. Water is needed for life and makes up most of the matter in a human body. Liquid water follows all of the typical rules for liquids, including taking the shape of its container, but has a constant mass and volume.

Mixture, Solution, and Colloid

A **mixture** is made of two or more substances that are combined in various proportions. The exact proportion of the constituents is the defining characteristic of any mixture. There are two types of mixtures: homogeneous and heterogeneous. **Homogeneous** means that the mixture's composition and properties are uniform throughout. Conversely, **heterogeneous** means that the mixture's composition and properties are not uniform throughout.

Solutions and Solubility

A **solution** is a homogeneous mixture of substances that cannot be separated by filtration or centrifugation. Solutions are made by dissolving one or more solutes into a solvent. For example, in a solution of sugar and water, sugar is the solute and water is the solvent. If there is more than one liquid present in the solution, then the most prevalent liquid is considered the solvent. The exact mechanism of dissolving varies depending on the mixture, but the result is always individual solute ions or molecules surrounded by solvent molecules. The proportion of solute to solvent for a particular solution is its **concentration**. Not all materials are able to be dissolved. Sugar is considered **soluble** in water, but sand does not dissolve in water, so it is considered **insoluble** in water.

A **colloid** is a heterogeneous mixture in which small particles (<1 micrometer) are suspended, but not dissolved, in a liquid. As such, they can be separated by centrifugation. A commonplace example of a colloid is milk.

Physical Properties of Mixtures and Solutions

When making a mixture or solution of ingredients, a person is not making a chemical change to the ingredients. Since the original ingredients are still present, their **physical properties** are usually still observable in the final mixture. Take, for instance, a solution of salt and water. The salt dissolves completely in the water, but since the salt is still present, the solution then tastes salty. Other properties, such as magnetism, do not transfer to the whole mixture. If a person were to mix sand and iron filings, then wave a magnet over the mixture, the iron filings would separate out, leaving only sand behind.

Acids and Bases and Water

One property of matter is called its pH value, which determines if a chemical is an **acid** or a **base**. Acids, such as lemon juice, tend to taste sour, whereas bases, such as soap, tend to feel slippery and taste bitter. Some chemicals, such as water, are called **neutral** because they are neither an acid or a base. Just like with other mixtures of ingredients with different properties, an acid or a base can be mixed with water to change the strength of the property. Lemon juice is very strong and sour to the taste at full strength, but when mixed with water and sugar, it can be sweet instead of sour. To add water to reduce the strength of a solution is called **dilution.**

	Very Acidic			**Neutral**			**Very Basic**
pH value	0-2	2-4	5-7	7	7-9	10-12	12-14
	Hydrochloric Acid and Stomach Acid	Vinegar, Fruit Juice, and Sodas	Tomatoes and Bananas	Water	Eggs and Baking Soda	Soap and Ammonia	Bleach and Drain Cleaner

Force, Motion, and Energy

GRAVITY

Gravity is a force that exists between all objects with matter. **Gravity** is a pulling force between objects, meaning that the forces on the objects point toward the opposite object. Gravity as we experience it is the force that the Earth exerts on objects, pulling them downward toward the center of the Earth. When Newton's third law is applied to gravity, the force pairs from gravity are shown to be equal in magnitude and opposite in direction.

Technically, all matter pulls other matter. The more massive the object, the more it pulls. The Earth is seen as our center of gravity because it is the most massive object nearby. Gravity is also reason that the Earth and other planets revolve around the Sun. The Sun is so massive that the Earth and all of the other bodies within the solar system are drawn to it and revolve around it as a result.

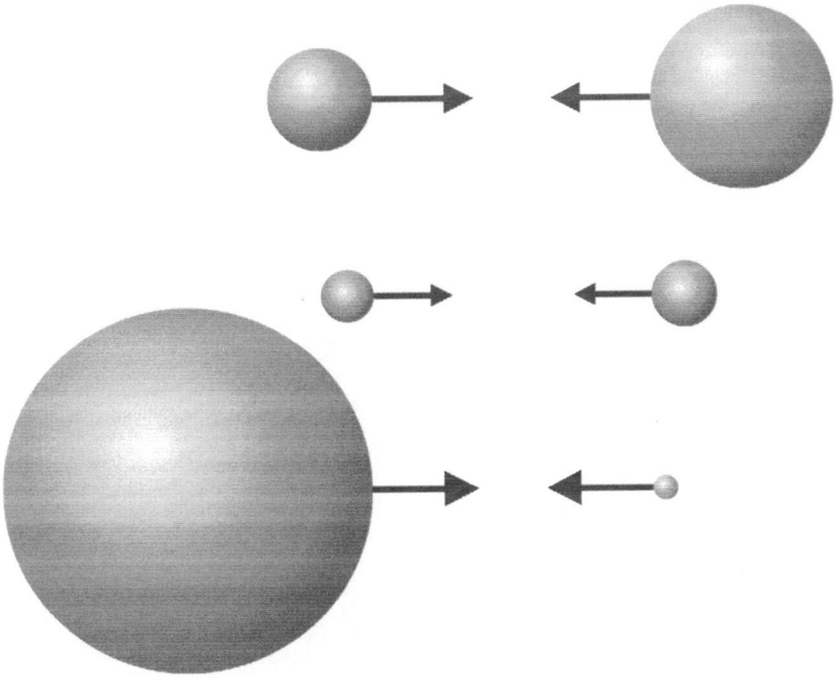

FRICTION

Friction is a resistance to motion between contacting surfaces. In order to illustrate the concept of friction, let us imagine a book resting on a table. As it sits, the force of its weight is equal to and opposite of the normal force. If, however, we were to exert a force on the book, attempting to push it to one side, a frictional force would arise, equal and opposite to our force. This kind of frictional force is known as static frictional force.

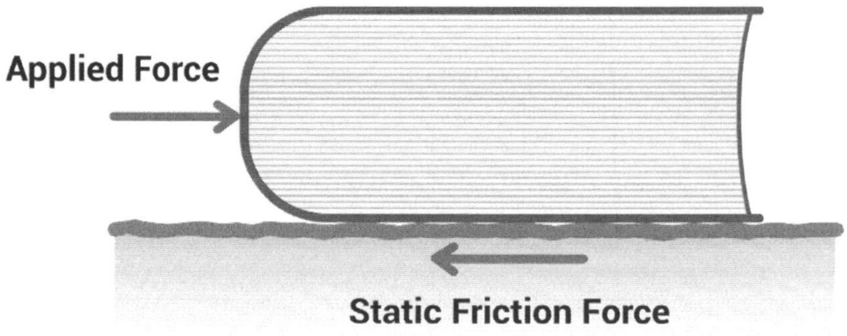

As we increase our force on the book, however, we will eventually cause it to accelerate in the direction of our force. At this point, the frictional force opposing us will be known as kinetic friction. For many combinations of surfaces, the magnitude of the kinetic frictional force is lower than that of the static frictional force, and consequently, the amount of force needed to maintain the movement of the book will be less than that needed to initiate the movement.

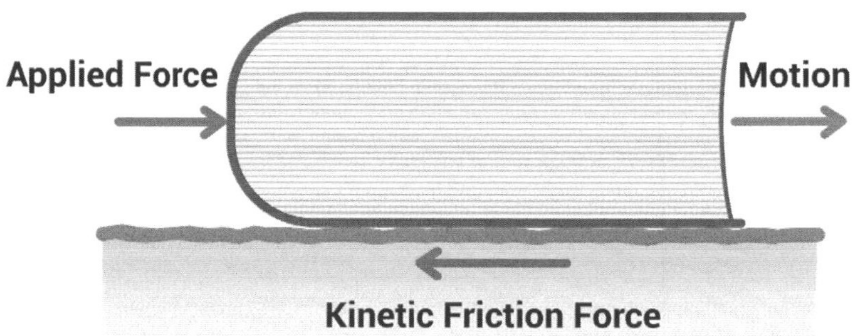

Review Video: Friction
Visit mometrix.com/academy and enter code: 716782

MAGNETISM

Magnetism is an **attraction** between opposite poles of **magnetic materials** and a **repulsion** between similar poles of magnetic materials. Magnetism can be natural or induced with the use of electric currents. Magnets almost always exist with two polar sides: north and south. A magnetic force exists between two poles on objects. Different poles attract each other. Like poles repel each other.

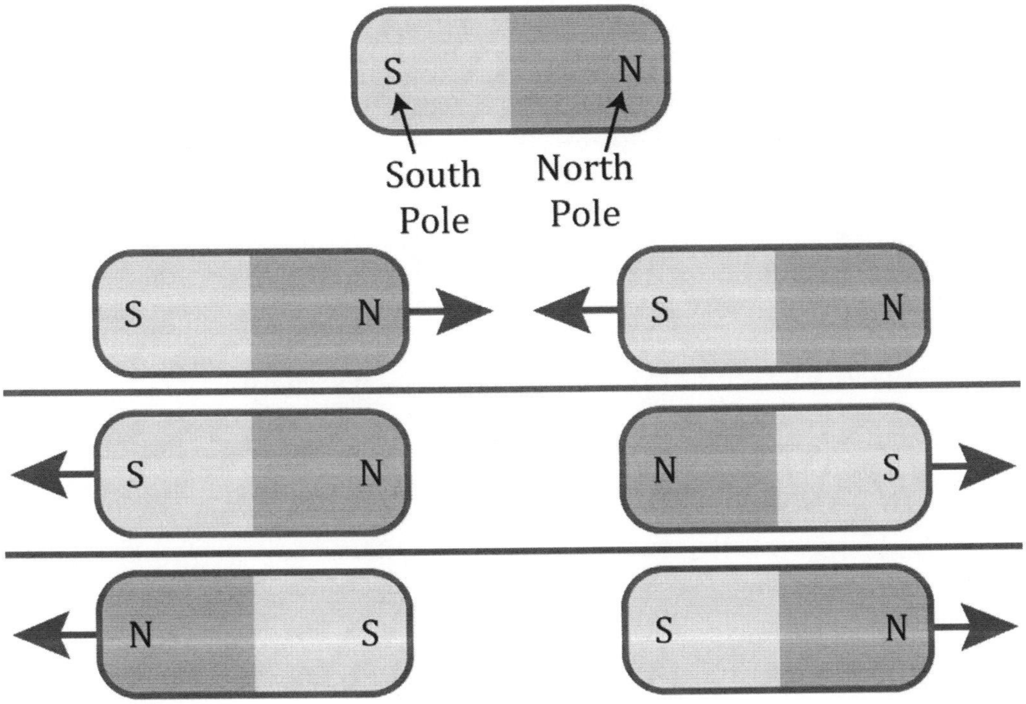

Speed and Velocity

Speed is a scalar quantity. That is, it has a **magnitude** but the **direction** does not matter. The formula for speed is the distance traveled within a certain amount of time. Velocity is a **vector quantity,** which means it has both magnitude and **direction**. For example, if you drive your car at a constant 70 kilometers per hour in any direction, you will be traveling at the **same speed**. Even if you drive around a curve and change your direction of travel, you are still traveling at the same speed as long as the car remains at 70 km/h. However, if you change your direction of travel, you have changed your velocity. **Velocity** is a specified speed in a specified direction. When you go around a corner in your car, even though you maintain the same speed, you have changed velocity because the direction has changed. Any change in velocity, such as a change in speed, direction, or both, constitutes acceleration and requires that a net unbalanced force act upon the moving system.

Acceleration

Acceleration is the **change in the velocity** of an object. Like velocity, acceleration may be computed as an average or an instantaneous quantity. To calculate average acceleration, we may use this simple equation: $a_{av} = \frac{v_f - v_i}{t_f - t_i}$, where the subscripts i and f denote the initial and final values of the velocity and time. The so-called instantaneous acceleration of an object can be found by reducing the time component to the limiting value until instantaneous velocity is approached. Acceleration will be expressed in units of distance divided by time squared; for instance, meters per second squared. Like position and velocity, acceleration is a vector quantity and will therefore have both magnitude and direction.

Examples of Newton's Laws in the Real World

- **Vehicle restraints** – seat belts and air bags all work to slow down the acceleration applied to the body in a car wreck. When a car hits another car, it slows down almost immediately, but the body and objects inside have inertia of their own, so they want to continue moving forward. Acceleration is directly related to force, so stopping immediately with the car would be harmful. Instead, the safety features help slow down the acceleration to keep the people inside safe.
- **Amusement park rides** – Rollercoasters apply Newton's laws in many ways. Rollercoasters tend to go very fast, but before you see them do so, they often climb a tall hill before falling very fast. In this way, they use gravity to their advantage to gain as much speed as possible before performing stunts like loop-the-loops and twists. Rollercoasters and other rides seem to defy gravity sometimes, making people feel like they are floating when they are only falling slower than the rollercoaster itself. If a rollercoaster goes down quickly, the body tries to stay in the air, causing this type of effect.
- **Earth's tectonic activities** – The theory of plate tectonics says that there are moving layers of the Earth's crust called plates. These plates are very slow moving, but enormous. When these plates bump into each other or slide past each other, they cause massive amounts of force because of Newton's laws. Every action produces an equal and opposite reaction. This is the cause of earthquakes, mountain volcano formation, and some forms of tidal waves.
- **Rocket launches** – When rockets are launched, many forces are at play. The rockets are huge, and they require a great amount of force to lift them into the air and into space. To do so, the rockets ignite fuel underneath and push downwards to cause lift upwards. These forces must be carefully calculated, however, so that the rocket does not veer off in the wrong direction and so that the humans and cargo inside don't accelerate fast enough that they are harmed in the process.

Motion and Force

Sir Isaac Newton observed three major laws explaining how the motion of an object works. The term **motion** refers to the movement of an object and the term **force** refers to physical energy that is applied to an object. Newton also referred to objects that are not moving as being in a state of **rest**.

- **Newton's First Law of Motion** - a body will remain at **rest** or in **motion** until a **force** is applied to it.
  - A bowling ball continues to roll in the same direction it was thrown until friction eventually slows it down.
  - A ball sitting on the ground will not move unless a force is applied to it.

- **Newton's Second Law of Motion** -the amount of **acceleration** is determined by the amount of **force** and the **mass** of the object being moved.
    - A soccer ball will accelerate more if kicked harder.

    - A shopping cart is much easier to push than a car because it is much less massive.

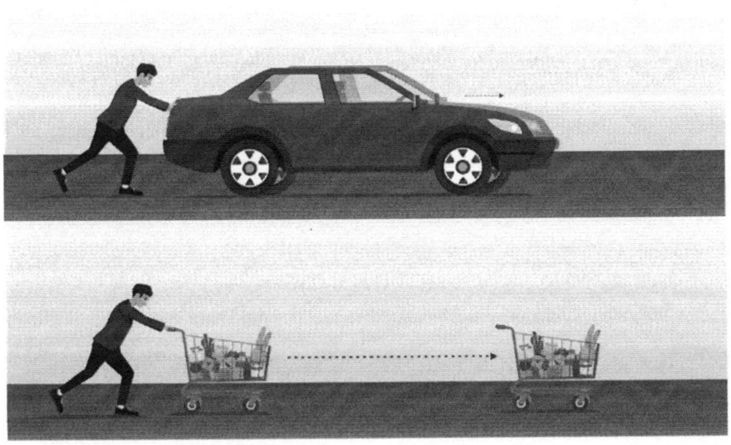

- **Newton's Third Law of Motion** – For every **action**, there is an equal and opposite **reaction**.
    - The floor applies force upward to hold up the weight of a person standing on it.
    - A dog pulls against a leash that his owner is holding.

Directions of Motion

Motion can be either linear, rotational, or oscillating.

- **Linear motion** - a single direction, like a bowling ball rolling down the lane or a train moving in one direction down its tracks.
- **Rotational motion** – rotating or spinning in a circular motion, such as a top spinning, a merry-go-round, or the Earth rotating around the Sun.
- **Oscillating motion** – bouncing up and down repeatedly, such as a yo-yo on a string or a spring. This also includes waves as they rise and fall.

Kinetic Energy

The **kinetic energy of an object** is that quality of its motion that can be related in a qualitative way to the amount of work performed on the object. Kinetic energy can be defined as $KE = mv^2/2$, in which m is the mass of an object and v is the magnitude of its velocity. Kinetic energy cannot be negative, since it depends on the square of velocity. Units for kinetic energy are the same as those for work: joules. Kinetic energy is a scalar quantity.

Changes in kinetic energy occur when a force does work on an object, such that the speed of the object is altered. This change in kinetic energy is equal to the amount of work that is done, and can be expressed as $W = KE_f - KE_i = \Delta KE$. This equation is commonly referred to as the work-kinetic energy theorem. If there are several different forces acting on the object, then W in this equation is simply the total work done by all the forces, or by the net force. This equation can be very helpful in solving some problems that would otherwise rely solely on Newton's laws of motion.

Potential Energy

Potential energy is the amount of energy that can be ascribed to a body or bodies based on configuration. There are a couple of different kinds of potential energy. **Gravitational potential energy** is the energy associated with the separation of bodies that are attracted to one another gravitationally. Any time you lift an object, you are increasing its gravitational potential energy. Gravitational potential energy can be found by the equation $PE = mgh$, where m is the mass of an object, g is the gravitational acceleration, and h is its height above a reference point, most often the ground.

Another kind of potential energy is **elastic potential energy**; elastic potential energy is associated with the compression or expansion of an elastic, or spring-like, object. Physicists will often refer to potential energy as being stored within a body, the implication being that it could emerge in the future.

Review Video: Potential and Kinetic Energy
Visit mometrix.com/academy and enter code: 491502

Mechanical Advantage

Simple machines include the inclined plane, lever, wheel and axle, and pulley. These simple machines have no internal source of energy. More complex or compound machines can be formed from them. Simple machines provide a mechanical advantage to make it easier to accomplish a task. The inclined plane enables a force less than the object's weight to be used to push an object to a greater height. A lever enables a multiplication of force. The wheel and axle allows for movement with less resistance. Single or double pulleys allow for easier direction of force. The wedge and screw are forms of the inclined plane. A wedge turns a smaller force working over a greater distance into a larger force. The screw is similar to an incline that is wrapped around a shaft.

Review Video: Simple Machines
Visit mometrix.com/academy and enter code: 950789

Inclined Planes

An **inclined plane** is a flat surface with one end raised higher than the other— like a ramp. It works similar to a lever. By pushing a heavy object over a longer distance (the inclined plane), the object can be raised a shorter distance in height with a smaller force than it would take to lift it straight up.

The longer the inclined plane, the less force is required to raise the object. This is also a simple machine.

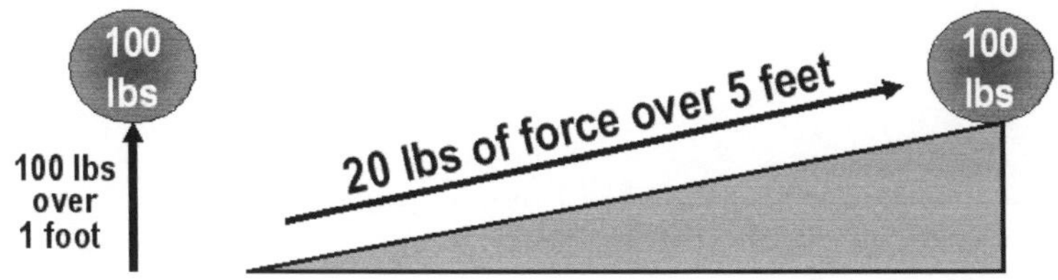

Levers

A **lever** is a simple machine made up of a rigid rod or beam that rotates on a fixed pivot or **fulcrum**. It can be used to lift a heavy mass by applying a small force over a large distance at one end to exert a much larger force over a shorter distance at the other end. Seesaws, crowbars, and shovels are all levers. Increasing the length of the lever arm decreases the necessary force required to lift the weight. A lever is a simple machine.

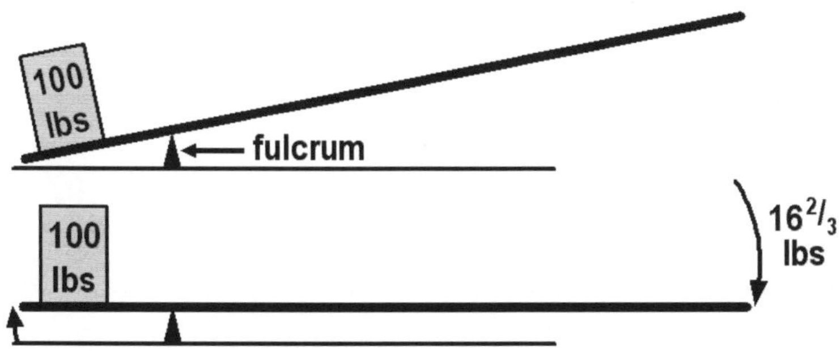

Screws

A screw is another kind of simple machine. It turns rotational force (the turning of the screw) into forward or linear force that makes the screw bore into wood or other substance. The screw is an inclined plane wrapped around a central nail. The force of turning the screw with a screwdriver acts along the longer distance of the spiral inclined plane to penetrate a shorter distance into the wood. It takes less force to turn the screw than to hammer a nail into the wood.

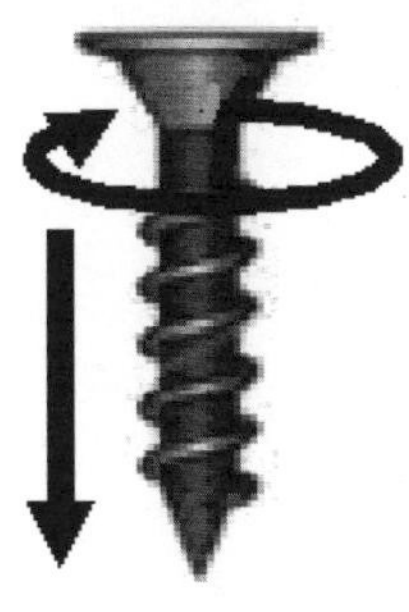

WEDGES

Still another kind of simple machine is a wedge, like an axe or a knife. A wedge concentrates and converts a downward force into a sideways force. It cuts down into an object and pushes the sections to the side. A nail is also a wedge.

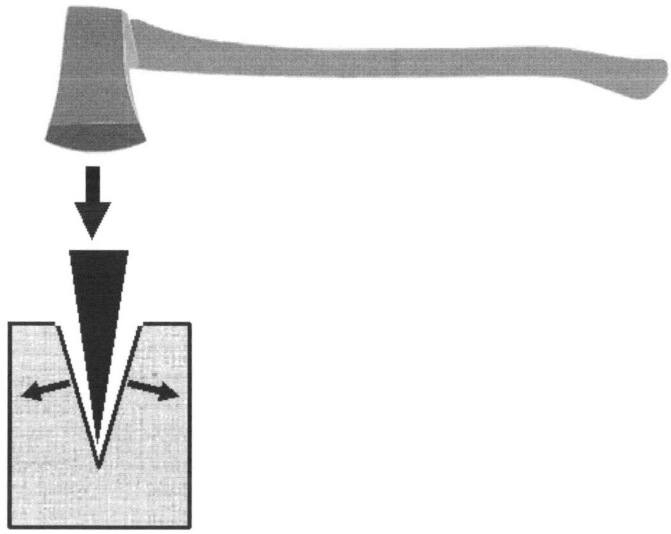

WHEELS AND AXLES

A wheel and axle is a type of simple machine. A wheel is basically a large circular lever attached to a much smaller axle. By applying a small force to turn the wheel a longer distance around the wheel, a much larger force is given to the smaller diameter axle. A doorknob is an example. The wider the knob the easier it is to open the door latch.

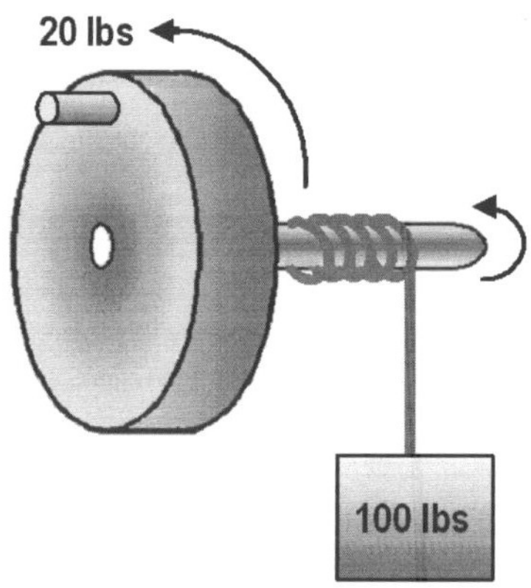

Review Video: Simple Machines - Wheel and Axle
Visit mometrix.com/academy and enter code: 574045

PULLEYS

A pulley is one or more wheels with grooved rims through which a rope or cable runs to change the direction of pull and lift a load. With just a single fixed pulley the amount of force needed to lift a weight is the same as the weight. But if a second moveable pulley is added as shown here, the amount of force needed to lift the weight is cut in half — just 50 pounds.

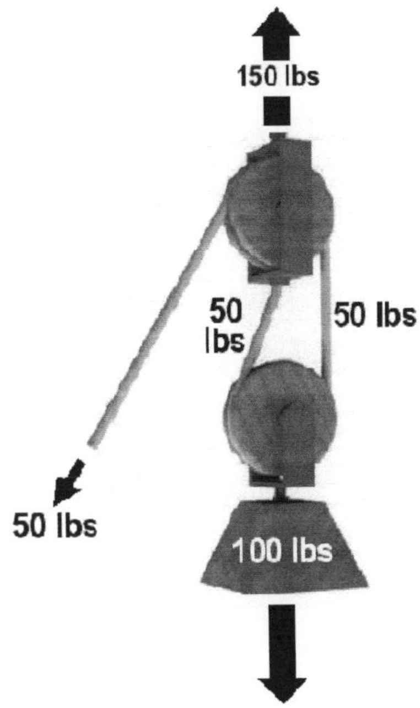

Liquid Water vs. Ice

There is a difference in state. The water in the glass is a liquid, while that in the pail is a solid. The liquid water flows and takes the shape of its container. The solid ice does not flow and does not assume the shape of the pail. The ice is also less dense than the water and will float in the water.

Complex Machines

A complex machine is a machine that combines two or more simple machines. For example a pair of scissors is made up of two wedges acting in opposite directions connected by a lever.

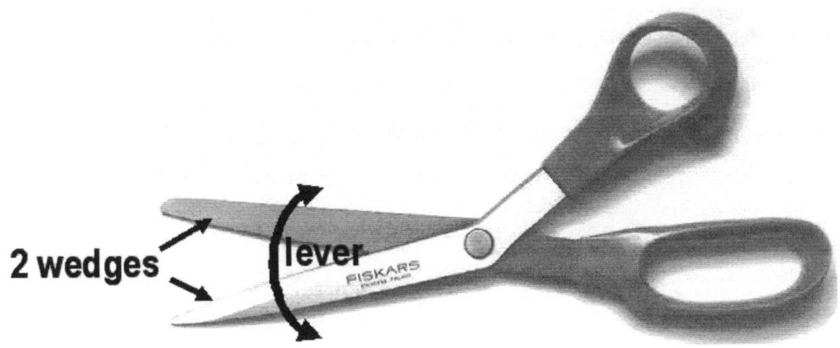

Wheelbarrows

A wheelbarrow is a complex machine. It is a lever mounted on a wheel and axle.

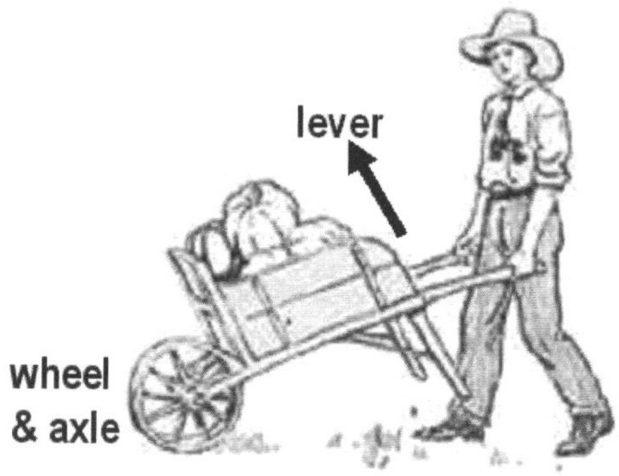

Saw

A saw is actually a complex machine. Each tooth in a saw blade is a wedge. Therefore, a saw consists of many wedges, which makes it a complex machine. When a person saws a piece of wood, he exerts both a downward force and a back and forth force. This cuts into the wood and pushes the two sides apart just like an axe.

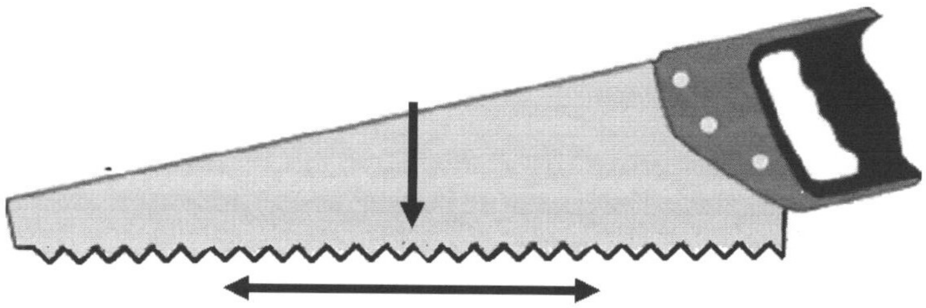

Earth and Space Science

Sun

The **Sun** is the vital force of life on Earth; it is also the central component of our solar system. It is basically a sphere of extremely hot gases (close to 15 million degrees at the core) held together by gravity. Some of these gaseous molecules are ionized due to the high temperatures. The balance between its gravitational force and the pressure produced by the hot gases is called **hydrostatic equilibrium**. The source of the solar energy that keeps the Sun alive and plays a key role in the perpetuation of life on Earth is located in the Sun's core, where nucleosynthesis produces heat energy and photons. The Sun's atmosphere consists of the photosphere, the surface visible from Earth, the chromosphere, a layer outside of and hotter than the photosphere, the transition zone (the region where temperatures rise between the chromosphere and the corona), and the corona, which is best viewed at x-ray wavelengths. A solar flare is an explosive emission of ionized particles from the Sun's surface.

Review Video: The Sun
Visit mometrix.com/academy and enter code: 699233

Earth's Rotation

The **Earth rotates** west to east about its axis, an imaginary straight line that runs nearly vertically through the center of the planet. This rotation (which takes 23 hours, 56 minutes, and 5 seconds) places each section of the Earth's surface in a position facing the Sun for a period of time, thus creating the alternating periods of light and darkness we experience as **day and night**. This rotation constitutes a sidereal day; it is measured as the amount of time required for a reference star to cross the meridian (an imaginary north-south line above an observer). Each star crosses the meridian once every (sidereal) day. Since the speed at which Earth rotates is not exactly constant, we use the mean solar day (a 24-hour period) in timekeeping rather than the slightly variable sidereal day.

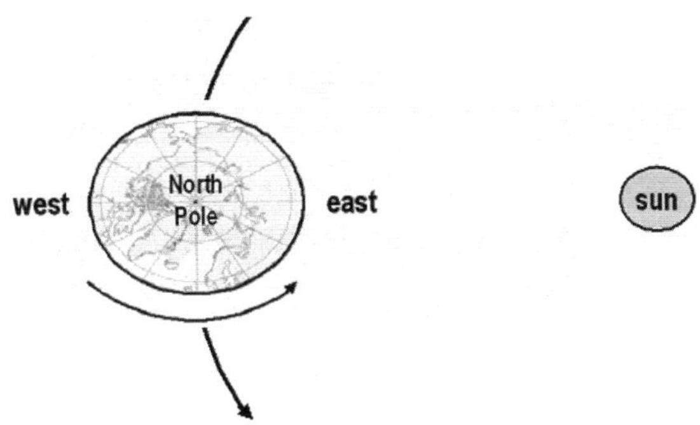

Earth's Revolution Around the Sun

Like all celestial objects in our solar system, planet **Earth** revolves around the **Sun**. This process takes approximately 365 1/4 days, the period of time that constitutes a calendar year. The path of the orbit of Earth around the Sun is not circular but **elliptical**. Therefore, the distances between the Earth and the Sun at points on either extreme of this counterclockwise orbit are not equal. In other words, the distance between the two objects varies over the course of a year. At **perihelion**, the minimum heliocentric distance, Earth is 147 million kilometers from the Sun. At **aphelion**, the maximum heliocentric distance, Earth is 152 million kilometers from the Sun. This movement of the

Earth is responsible for the apparent annual motions of the Sun (in a path referred to as the ecliptic) and other celestial objects visible from Earth's surface.

Review Video: Astronomy
Visit mometrix.com/academy and enter code: 640556

Review Video: The Solar System
Visit mometrix.com/academy and enter code: 273231

Moon

Earth's Moon is historically one of the most studied celestial bodies. Its mass is approximately 1.2% of the Earth's mass, and its radius is just over one-fourth of the size of the Earth's radius. Measurements of the Moon's density suggest that its characteristics are similar to those of the rocks that make up Earth's crust. The **landscape** of the Moon consists mostly of mountains and craters formed by collisions of this surface with meteors and other interplanetary materials. The Moon's crust (estimated to be 50 to 100 kilometers in thickness) is made up of a layer of regolith (lunar soil) supported by a layer of loose rocks and gravel. Beneath the crust is a mantle made up of a solid lithosphere and a semiliquid asthenosphere. The Moon's **core** (the innermost 500 kilometers of the body) is not as dense as that of the Earth. The Moon is made up mostly of refractory elements with high melting and boiling points with low levels of heavy elements such as iron.

Formation Theories

The **fission model** of Moon origin suggests that the Moon is actually a piece of the Earth that split off early during the planet's formation. In this model, a portion of the Earth's mantle fissioned off during a liquid stage in its formation, creating the Moon. According to the **capture model**, the Moon formed elsewhere in the solar system and was subsequently captured by the Earth's gravitational field. The **double-impact model** states that the Earth and the Moon formed during the same period of time from the same accretion material. Each of these theories has its strengths, but none of them can explain all of the properties of the Moon and its relationship to the Earth. Recently, a fourth (widely accepted) hypothesis has been suggested, which involves the **collision** between the Earth and a large asteroid. This hypothetical collision is said to have released a large amount of Earth's crustal material into its orbit; the Moon accreted from that material and the material displaced from the asteroid due to the collision.

Earth-Moon System

While the Moon is commonly referred to as a satellite of the Earth, this is not entirely accurate. The ratio of the masses of the two bodies is much larger than that of any other planet-satellite system. Also, the Moon does not truly **revolve** around the Earth. Rather, the two bodies revolve around a common center of mass beneath the surface of the Earth (approximately 4,800 kilometers from Earth's core). The **orbital planes** of the Moon and the Earth are nearly aligned; therefore, the Moon moves close to the ecliptic, as seen from Earth. Due to the Moon's synchronous rotation (its rotation period and orbital period are equal); the same side of the Moon is always facing Earth. This occurs because of the **mutual gravitational pull** between the two bodies. These mutual gravitational pulls play a role in changing the ocean tides as well. The moon pulls the oceanic waters toward itself, causing high tide in the side closest to the moon and low tides in areas further from the moon.

Phases

The **sidereal period** of the Moon (the time it takes the Moon to orbit the Earth with the fixed stars as reference points) is about 27 days. The **lunar month** (or synodic period) is the period of time required for the Moon to return to a given alignment as observed from the Earth with the Sun as a reference point; this takes 29 days, 12 hours, 44 minutes, and 28 seconds. A discrepancy exists between the two periods of time because the Earth and the Moon move at the same time. Sunlight reflected off of the Moon's surface at different times during the lunar month causes its apparent shape to change. The sequence of the Moon's shapes is referred to as the **phases of the Moon**. The full Moon can be viewed when the body is directly opposite from the Sun. The opposite end of the cycle, the new Moon, occurs when the Moon is not visible from Earth because it is situated between the Earth and the Sun.

CONFIGURATIONS

The **configurations of the Moon** describe its position with respect to the Earth and the Sun. We can thus observe a correlation between the phases of the Moon and its configuration. The Moon is at **conjunction** at the time of the new Moon—it is situated in the same direction as the Sun. **Quadrature** (which signals the first quarter phase) is the position of the Moon at a right angle between the Earth-Sun line; we see exactly half of the Moon's sunlit hemisphere. This is the **waxing crescent phase**, in which we see more of the Moon each night. Then comes opposition (which occurs when the Moon lies in the direction opposite the Sun)—we see the full Moon. After this point, the Moon enters its **waning gibbons phase** as it travels back toward quadrature. When it reaches that point again, it has entered the third-quarter phase. Finally, as the Moon circles back toward conjunction, it is in its waning crescent phase.

PHASES OF THE MOON

As the moon revolves around Earth approximately every 27.3 days, light from the Sun hits it from different angles. This causes the Moon to be in full sunlight (full moon) when Earth is between it and the Sun, complete darkness (new moon) when it is between Earth and the Sun, and all stages in between. When the Moon is half in sunlight and half in shadow it is in the first or last quarter, depending on whether it is heading towards becoming a full moon or a new moon.

Review Video: Moon
Visit mometrix.com/academy and enter code: 880415

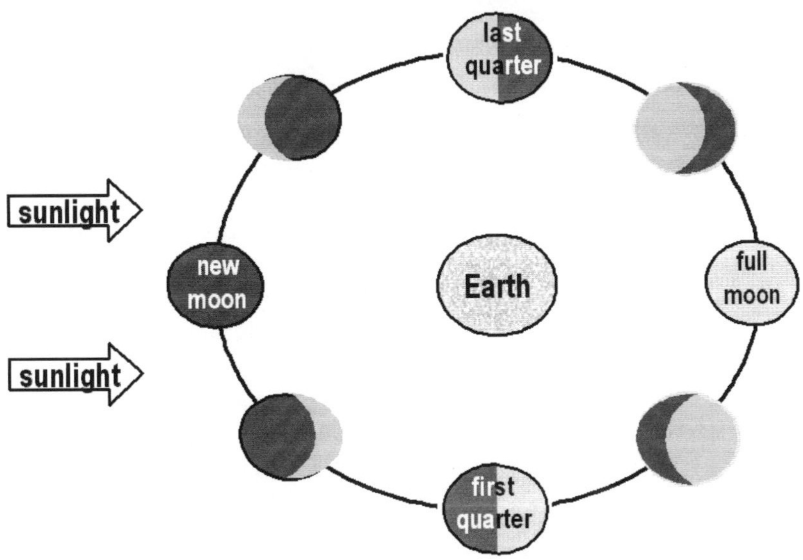

EARTH'S ATMOSPHERE

Earth's gravity is strong enough to attract the molecules of the gases in the atmosphere and keep them in a layer surrounding the planet. The gravity of smaller celestial bodies like Mercury and

Earth's moon is not strong enough to do this, and their atmospheres long ago diffused out into space.

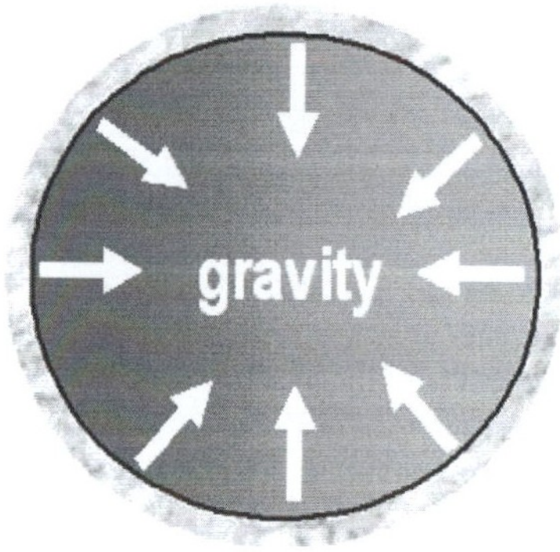

Seasons

Earth is tilted on its axis as it revolves around the Sun and rotates upon its axis from left to right. That means more sunshine and longer days and shorter nights in the hemisphere facing the Sun. More sunlight means warmer temperatures. In the left-hand picture the Southern Hemisphere is experiencing its summer. Six months later when Earth is on the opposite side of the Sun it is the Northern Hemisphere that is having summer.

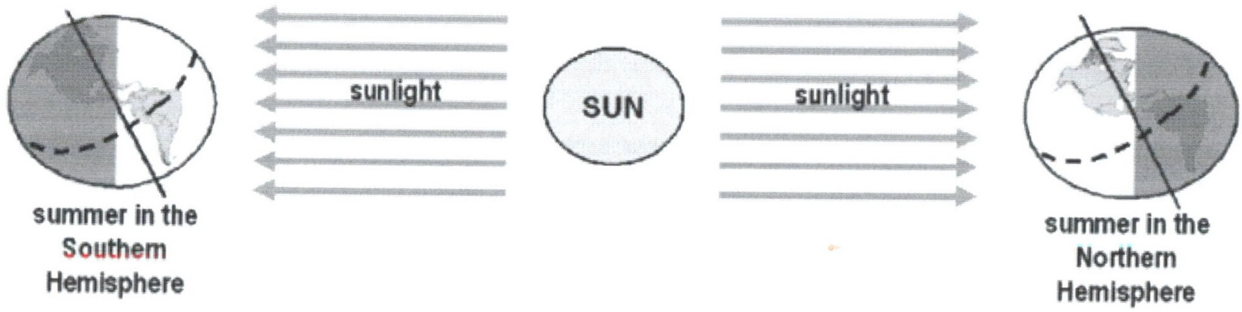

Eclipses

Eclipses occur when one celestial body obscures the view of another, either partially or completely. A **solar eclipse**, or eclipse of the Sun by the Moon, happens when the Moon passes directly in front of the Sun (as observed from Earth). Alternately, a **lunar eclipse** occurs when the Moon is situated in the Earth's shadow and is therefore completely invisible. These events do not happen every month because of the differential between the orbital planes of the Moon and the Earth—the Moon's orbit is about five degrees off from the ecliptic. The Moon's orbital path is subject to the same precession that occurs in the Earth's rotational axis; this causes the occasional intersection of the orbital planes of the two bodies. Therefore, eclipses are produced by a combination of the effects of the precession of the Moon's orbit, the orbit itself, and the Earth's orbit.

Solar System

The *solar system* consists of the sun and eight *major planets*. In order from the sun the planets are Mercury, Venus, Earth, Mars, Jupiter, Saturn, Uranus and Neptune. Pluto is no longer considered to be a major planet. Along with 5 other similar sized objects it is now a *minor planet*. Six of the major planets have one or more moons. The solar system also contains countless *meteoroids, asteroids*, and *comets*.

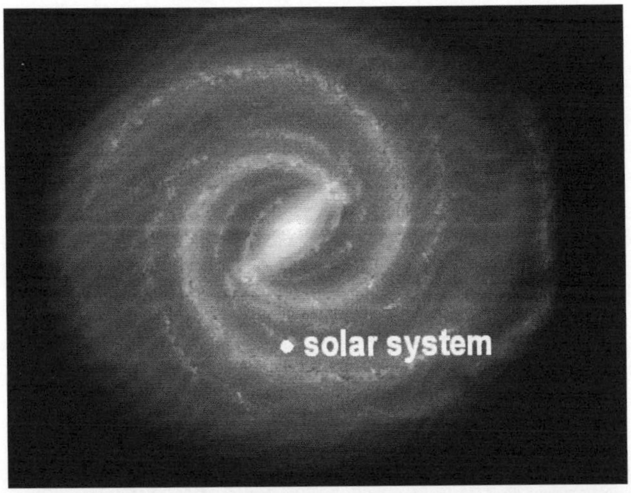

TERRESTRIAL PLANETS

The term **terrestrial planets** refers to the four planets closest to the Sun (Mercury, Venus, Earth, and Mars). They are classified together because they share many similarities that distinguish them from the giant planets. The terrestrial planets have **high densities and atmospheres** that constitute a small percentage of their total masses. These atmospheres consist mostly of heavy elements, such as carbon dioxide, nitrogen, and water, and are maintained by the gravitational field of the planets (which could not prevent hydrogen from escaping). These planets exhibit magnetic fields of varying intensity. An important characteristic that distinguishes the terrestrial planets from the giant planets is the evidence of various levels of internally generated activity, which caused these planets to evolve from their original states. These processes are thought to have been caused by constant meteoritic impacts during the first few hundred million years of the planets' existence. Radioactive decay of certain isotopes increased the internal temperatures of these planets, leading to volcanic activity on all of the terrestrial planets except Venus.

MERCURY

Mercury, the smallest interior planet, is the least well known of the four. This is due to its close proximity to the Sun and high temperatures. Mercury's atmosphere is not very dense; this means that the planet's surface experiences wide temperature differentials from day to night. Mercury's density is close to that of Earth. As the smallest planet known to have experienced planetary evolution, Mercury's internal activity ceased (it became extinct) thousands of millions of years ago. The size of the planet is relevant because less massive bodies cool more quickly than larger ones after cessation of radioactivity. Mercury's surface is characterized by craters produced by meteoritic impact.

Venus

Venus is comparable to Earth in both mass and density. Venus is the brightest planet in the sky (partially due to the fact that it is proximate to the Sun), which makes exploration of its surface difficult. This planet's atmosphere consists mainly of carbon dioxide, with trace amounts of water and carbon oxide molecules, as well as high levels of sulfuric, nitric, and hydrofluoric acids in the clouds that characterize this atmosphere. The concentration of clouds, coupled with the chemical makeup of Venus's atmosphere, result in a strong greenhouse effect at the planet's surface. This surface consists of large plains (thought to be created by either volcanic activity, which remains unproven, or by meteoritic impacts) and large impact craters. The materials that compose Venus's surface are highly radioactive. Some astronomers have suggested past single-plate tectonic activity; again, however, the planet's dense atmosphere makes valid surface observation quite difficult.

Mars

Mars and Earth exhibit many similarities. For example, Mars has an internal structure that includes a central metallic core, a mantle rich in olivine and iron oxide, and a crust of hydrated silicates. Martian soil consists largely of basalts and clay silicate, with elements of sulfur, silicon oxide, and iron oxide. The planet's surface belies high levels of past volcanic activity (though, due to its relatively small mass, it is probably extinct). In fact, Mars is home to the largest known volcano in the solar system. The Martian landscape also includes two major basins, ridges and plateaus, and, most notably, apparent evidence of fluvial (water-based) erosion landforms, such as canyons and canals. It is possible that the past pressures and temperatures on Mars allowed water to exist on the red planet. Some have gone so far as to suggest that this planet was a site of biochemical evolution. So far, however, no evidence of life has been found.

Mars's Satellites

Two Martian satellites have been observed: **Phobos** and **Deimos**. Each of these bodies is ellipsoidal; the circular orbits of the two satellites lie in Mars's equatorial plane. The gravitational forces between this planet and Phobos and Deimos have caused both satellites to settle into synchronous rotation (the same parts of their surfaces are always facing Mars). This feature exerts a braking force on Phobos's orbit. In other words, its orbit is decreasing in size. The relationship between Deimos and Mars is similar to the Earth-Moon system, in which the radius of the satellite's orbit is gradually growing. The differential compositions and densities of Mars and its satellites indicate that Phobos and Deimos probably did not break off from Mars.

Giant Planets

The **large diameters** of Jupiter, Saturn, Uranus, and Neptune gave rise to the name of the category into which they fall. The **hypothetical icy cores** of these planets cause them to exhibit primary atmospheres, because the large levels of mass they accreted prevented even the lightest elements from escaping their gravitational pulls. The atmospheres of the giant planets thus consist mostly of hydrogen and helium. The giant planets do not have solid surfaces like those of the terrestrial planets. Jupiter probably consists of a core (made of ice and rock) surrounded by a layer of metallic hydrogen, which is covered by a convective atmosphere of hydrogen and helium. Saturn is believed to have the same type of core and hydrogen mantle, enriched by the helium missing from the atmosphere, surrounded by a differentiation zone and a hydrogenic atmosphere. Uranus and Neptune probably have the same type of core, surrounded by ionic materials, bounded by methane-rich molecular envelopes. Uranus is the only giant planet that exhibits no evidence of internal activity.

Rings

Each of the four giant planets exhibits **rings**. These are flat disks of fragmented material that orbit just next to their respective planets. Many of the giant planets' smaller satellites are embedded in these rings. There are two main hypotheses regarding the formation of such rings. One theory suggests that the tidal force exerted on a satellite by its planet may surpass the **Roche limit** (the point at which particle cohesion is no longer possible) and break the satellite into fragments, which then collide and become smaller. This material then spreads out and forms a ring. An alternate theory of the formation of the rings of the giant planets suggests that there was unaccreted material left over after the formation of these planets. Below the Roche limit (within a certain vicinity to the planet), these particles could not join together to form satellites and would consequently settle into orbital rings.

Satellites

Each of the giant planets possesses a number of **satellites. Jupiter** has over 50 known satellites—they are grouped according to size. Each of the four largest satellites of Jupiter exhibits evidence of internal activity at some point in their evolutions. In fact, Io, the densest satellite and the one closest to Jupiter, is the only celestial body besides Earth known to be currently volcanically active. **Saturn** has 21 satellites. Titan, the second-largest known satellite, has its own atmosphere. The other six largest of Saturn's satellites all have icy surfaces; some of these show evidence of past internal activity. The smaller 14 are relatively unknown. **Uranus** has five satellites. Each of them displays evidence of geological activity, in the form of valleys, smoothed surfaces, cliffs, mountains, and depressions. **Neptune** has eight known satellites. The larger, Triton, is similar to Titan in that it has an atmosphere. The other seven satellites of Neptune are relatively unknown.

Review Video: Giant Planets
Visit mometrix.com/academy and enter code: 563115

Pluto and Charon

Though Charon was originally considered a satellite of Pluto, it now appears that the two are more accurately described as a double dwarf planet system (largely because of the similarity in the sizes of the two and the recurring debate over how Pluto should be classified). It is believed that these bodies formed from the solar nebula like most other objects in the solar system. Pluto has a highly irregular orbit, which places it closer to the Sun than Neptune for periods of time. In sharp contrast to its giant neighbors, this planet's density is higher than that of water ice. The surface of Pluto consists of high levels of methane absorbed into ice, with trace amounts of carbon oxide and nitrogen. Charon resembles the major Uranian satellites more so than it does Pluto. It consists of water ice with a siliceous or hydrocarbonate contaminant.

Review Video: Pluto and Charon
Visit mometrix.com/academy and enter code: 426296

Milky Way

On a clear dark moonless night far from city lights a broad white band of stars that stretches across the sky can be seen. This is the Milky Way galaxy, and our sun and the solar system are part of it.

The Milky Way is a huge flat disk containing between 200 billion and 400 billion stars. Because Earth is in that disk, we see it edge on, which is why it appears to us as a broad band of light.

The Milky Way is a flat, disk-shaped spiral galaxy with a central bar-like bulge of stars. It is huge—between 100,000 and 120,000 light-years in diameter. A light-year is a unit of distance, not time. It is the distance light travels in one year, about 6 trillion miles. The Milky Way is between 600 thousand trillion and 700 thousand trillion miles across. Our solar system lies about two thirds of the way out on one of the spiral arms.

Stellar Observation

The observation of stars relates to one of three stellar properties: position, brightness, and spectra. **Positional stellar observation** is principally performed through study of the positions of stars on multiple photographic plates. Historically, this type of analysis was done through measurement of the angular positions of the stars in the sky. **Parallax** of a star is its apparent shift in position due to the revolution of the Earth about the Sun; this property can be used to establish the distance to a star. Observation of the **brightness** of a star involves the categorization of stars according to their magnitudes. There is a fixed intensity ratio between each of the six magnitudes. Since stars emit light over a range of wavelengths, viewing a star at different wavelengths can give an indication of its temperature. The analysis of stars' **spectra** provides information about the temperatures of stars—the higher a star's temperature, the more ionized the gas in its outer layer. A star's spectrum also relates to its chemical composition.

Binary Star

Binary star systems, of which about fifty percent of the stars in the sky are members, consist of two stars that orbit each other. The orbits of and distances between members of a binary system vary. A **visual binary** is a pair of stars that can be visually observed. Positional measurements of a visual binary reveal the orbital paths of the two stars. Astronomers can identify astrometric binaries through long-term observation of a visible star—if the star appears to wobble, it may be inferred that it is orbiting a companion star that is not visible. An **eclipsing binary** can be identified through observation of the brightness of a star. Variations in the visual brightness of a star can occur when one star in a binary system passes in front of the other. Sometimes, variations in the spectral lines of a star occur because it is in a binary system. This type of binary is a spectroscopic binary.

Review Video: Types of Stars
Visit mometrix.com/academy and enter code: 831934

Hertzsprung-Russell Diagram

The **Hertzsprung-Russell (H-R) diagram** was developed to explore the relationships between the luminosities and spectral qualities of stars. This diagram involves plotting these qualities on a graph, with absolute magnitude (luminosity) on the vertical and spectral class on the horizontal. Plotting a number of stars on the H-R diagram demonstrates that stars fall into narrowly defined regions, which correspond to stages in stellar evolution. Most stars are situated in a diagonal strip that runs from the top-left (high temperature, high luminosity) to the lower-right (low temperature, low luminosity). This diagonal line shows stars in the main sequence of evolution (often called dwarfs). Stars that fall above this line on the diagram (low temperature, high luminosity) are believed to be much larger than the stars on the main sequence (because their high luminosities are not due to higher temperatures than main sequence stars); they are termed giants and supergiants. Stars below the main sequence (high temperature, low luminosity) are called white dwarfs. The H-R diagram is useful in calculating distances to stars.

Stellar Evolution

The life cycle of a star is closely related to its **mass**—low-mass stars become white dwarfs, while high-mass stars become **supernovae**. A star is born when a **protostar** is formed from a **collapsing interstellar cloud**. The temperature at the center of the protostar rises, allowing nucleosynthesis to begin. **Nucleosynthesis**, or hydrogen-burning through fusion, entails a release of energy. Eventually, the star runs out of fuel (hydrogen). If the star is relatively low mass, the disruption of hydrostatic equilibrium allows the star to contract due to gravity. This raises the temperature just outside the core to a point at which nucleosynthesis and a different kind of fusion (with helium as fuel) that produces a carbon nucleus can occur. The star swells with greater energy, becoming a red giant. Once this phase is over, gravity becomes active again, shrinking the star until the degeneracy pressure of electrons begins to operate, creating a white dwarf that will eventually burn out. If the star has a high mass, the depletion of hydrogen creates a supernova.

Electromagnetic Spectrum

The **electromagnetic spectrum** is the range of all wavelengths and frequencies of known electromagnetic waves. Visible light occupies only a small portion of the electromagnetic spectrum. Some of the common classifications of electromagnetic waves are listed in the table below with their approximate frequency ranges.

Classification	Freq. (Hz)
Gamma Rays	$\sim 10^{19}$
X-Rays	$\sim 10^{17} - 10^{18}$
Ultraviolet	$\sim 10^{15} - 10^{16}$
Visible Light	$\sim 10^{14}$
Infra-red	$\sim 10^{11} - 10^{14}$
Microwaves	$\sim 10^{10} - 10^{11}$
Radio/TV	$\sim 10^{6} - 10^{9}$

Electromagnetic waves travel at the speed of light, $c = 3 \times 10^8$ m/s. To find the wavelength of any electromagnetic wave, simply divide c by the frequency. Visible light occupies a range of wavelengths from approximately 380 nm (violet) to 740 nm (red). The full spectrum of color can be found between these two wavelengths.

Review Video: Electromagnetic Spectrum
Visit mometrix.com/academy and enter code: 771761

Review Video: Light
Visit mometrix.com/academy and enter code: 900556

SUPERNOVA

When a star on the main sequence runs out of hydrogen fuel, it begins to burn helium (the by-product of nucleosynthesis). Once helium-burning is complete in a massive star, the mass causes the core temperature to rise, enabling the fusion of carbon, then silicon, and a succession of other atomic nuclei, each of which takes place in a new shell further out of the core. When the fusion cycle reaches iron (which cannot serve as fuel for a nuclear reaction), an iron core begins to form, which accumulates over time. Eventually, the temperature and pressure in the core become high enough for electrons to interact with protons in the iron nuclei to produce neutrons. In a matter of moments, this reaction is complete. The core falls and collides with the star's outer envelope, causing a massive explosion (a supernova). This continues until the neutrons exert degeneracy pressure; this creates a pulsar. In more massive stars, nothing can stop the collapse, which ends in the creation of a black hole.

COMET

Comets are small icy bodies ranging in size from tens of yards to tens of miles in diameter. They orbit the sun with periods of a few years to hundreds of thousands of years. Halley's comet shown here orbits the sun every 75 to 76 years. As a comet nears the sun a long tail or coma is created as ice and dust are blown off by the intense radiation and the solar wind of charged particles from the sun.

METEOROIDS AND METEORS

A *meteoroid* is a sand- to boulder-sized piece of debris hurtling through the solar system at speeds of between 15 and 45 miles per second. When it enters earth's atmosphere it burns up and leaves a visible fiery trail of gas and debris called a *meteor*. Some meteoroids are large enough that they do not completely burn up, and what remains reaches the ground. These are called *meteorites.* Meteoroids can be small pieces that have broken off of *asteroids.*

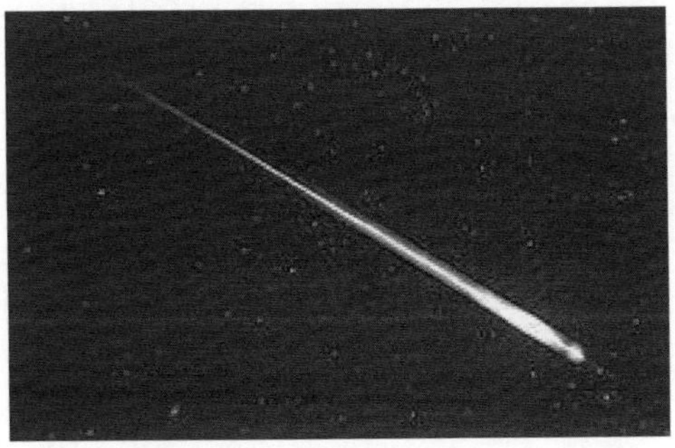

Asteroid

An **asteroid** is a small, solid planet (planetoid) that orbits the Sun. The orbital paths of most asteroids are between the orbits of Jupiter and Mars. Many of these bodies have been studied extensively and given names; those in the main belt (which tend to be carbonaceous) are classified into subgroups based on their distance from a large, named asteroid (for example, Floras, Hildas, Cybeles). **Atens** are asteroids whose orbits lie between the Earth and the Sun, and Apollos are asteroids with orbits that mimic Earth's. Asteroids may also be classified based on their composition. **C-type** asteroids exhibit compositions similar to that of the Sun and are fairly dark. S-type asteroids are made up of nickel-iron and iron- and magnesium-silicates; these are relatively bright. **Bright asteroids** made up exclusively of nickel-iron are classified as M-type. Observation of the relative brightness of an asteroid allows astronomers to estimate its size.

Plate Tectonics

Main Concepts

Plate tectonics is a geological theory that was developed to explain the process of continental drift. The theoretical separation of the Earth's lithosphere and asthenosphere is based upon the mechanical properties of the materials in the two respective layers and is distinct from the chemical separation of Earth's crust, mantle, and core. According to the theory of plate tectonics, the Earth's lithosphere is divided into **ten major plates**: African, Antarctic, Australian, Eurasian, North American, South American, Pacific, Cocos, Nazca, and Indian; it floats atop the asthenosphere. The plates of the lithosphere abut one another at plate boundaries (divergent, convergent, or transform fault), where the formation of topological features of Earth's surface begins.

Theory

This theory of plate tectonics arose from the fusion of **continental drift** (first proposed in 1915 by Alfred Wegener) and **seafloor spreading** (first observed by Icelandic fishermen in the 1800s and later refined by Harry Hess and Robert Dietz in the early 1960s) in the late 1960s and early 1970s. Prior to this time, the generally accepted explanation for continental drift was that the continents were floating on the Earth's oceans. The discovery that mountains have "roots" (proved by George Airy in the early 1950s) did not categorically disprove the concept of floating continents; scientists were still uncertain as to where those mountainous roots were attached. It was not until the identification and study of the Mid-Atlantic Ridge and magnetic striping in the 1960s that plate tectonics became accepted as a scientific theory. Its conception was a landmark event in the field of Earth sciences—it provided an explanation for the empirical observations of continental drift and seafloor spreading.

Tectonic Plate Motion

The two main sources of **tectonic plate motion** are **gravity** and **friction**. The energy driving tectonic plate motion comes from the dissipation of heat from the mantle in the relatively weak asthenosphere. This energy is converted into gravity or friction to incite the motion of plates. Gravity is subdivided by geologists into ridge-push and slab-pull. In the phenomenon of **ridge-push**, the motion of plates is instigated by the energy that causes low-density material from the mantle to rise at an oceanic ridge. This leads to the situation of certain plates at higher elevations; gravity causes material to slide downhill. In **slab-pull**, plate motion is thought to be caused by cold, heavy plates at oceanic trenches sinking back into the mantle, providing fuel for future convection. Friction is subdivided into mantle drag and trench suction. Mantle drag suggests that plates move due to the friction between the lithosphere and the asthenosphere. Trench suction involves a downward frictional pull on oceanic plates in subduction zones due to convection currents.

Review Video: Plate Tectonic Theory
Visit mometrix.com/academy and enter code: 535013

Plate Tectonics

Earthquakes result from the movement of a dozen or so major lithospheric (crustal) plates that float upon Earth's mantle (asthenosphere). These **plates** move about each other in response to complex convection cells set in motion by Earth's interior heat. Two plates move apart from each other at divergent boundaries, or spreading centers, and come together at convergent boundaries. When thin, denser, iron- and magnesium- rich oceanic crust collides with thicker, lighter, silica-rich continental crust, the former is subducted beneath the latter. The subducted material carries scraped-off continental crust and seawater down with it. As this material melts, it rises as a mixture of magma and steam to produce explosive volcanic mountain ranges such as those surrounding the Pacific Ocean Basin. When two continental plates collide at convergent boundaries, the crust buckles and thrusts up massive mountain ranges such as the Alps and Himalayas.

Rock Cycle

The **rock cycle** is the process whereby the materials that make up the Earth transition through the three types of rock: igneous, sedimentary, and metamorphic. Rocks, like all matter, cannot be created or destroyed; rather, they undergo a series of changes and adopt different forms through the functions of the rock cycle. Plate tectonics and the water cycle are the driving forces behind the rock cycle; they force rocks and minerals out of equilibrium and force them to adjust to different external conditions. Viewed in a generalized, cyclical fashion, the rock cycle operates as follows: rocks beneath Earth's surface melt into magma. This **magma** either erupts through volcanoes or remains inside the Earth. Regardless, the magma cools, forming igneous rocks. On the surface, these rocks experience **weathering** and **erosion**, which break them down and distribute the fragments across the surface. These fragments form layers and eventually become **sedimentary rocks**. Sedimentary rocks are then either transformed to **metamorphic rocks** (which will become magma inside the Earth) or melted down into magma.

Rock Formation

Igneous Rocks: Igneous rocks can be formed from sedimentary rocks, metamorphic rocks, or other igneous rocks. Rocks that are pushed under the Earth's surface (usually due to plate subduction) are exposed to high mantle temperatures, which cause the rocks to melt into magma. The magma then rises to the surface through volcanic processes. The lower atmospheric temperature causes the magma to cool, forming grainy, extrusive igneous rocks. The creation of extrusive, or volcanic, rocks is quite rapid. The cooling process can occur so rapidly that crystals do not form; in this case, the result is a glass, such as obsidian. It is also possible for magma to cool down inside the Earth's interior; this type of igneous rock is called intrusive. Intrusive, or plutonic, rocks cool more slowly, resulting in a coarse-grained texture.

Sedimentary Rocks: Sedimentary rocks are formed when rocks at the Earth's surface experience weathering and erosion, which break them down and distribute the fragments across the surface. Fragmented material (small pieces of rock, organic debris, and the chemical products of mineral sublimation) is deposited and accumulates in layers, with top layers burying the materials beneath. The pressure exerted by the topmost layers causes the lower layers to compact, creating solid sedimentary rock in a process called lithification.

Metamorphic Rocks: Metamorphic rocks are igneous or sedimentary rocks that have "morphed" into another kind of rock. In metamorphism, high temperatures and levels of pressure change preexisting rocks physically and/or chemically, which produces different species of rocks. In the rock cycle, this process generally occurs in materials that have been thrust back into the Earth's mantle by plate subduction. Regional metamorphism refers to a large band of metamorphic activity; this often occurs near areas of high orogenic (mountain-building) activity. Contact metamorphism refers to metamorphism that occurs when "country rock" (that is, rock native to an area) comes into contact with high-heat igneous intrusions (magma).

Formation of Deltas, Canyons, and Dunes

A **delta** is landform that is created at the mouth of a river, where it flows into a larger body of water. The river carries sediment and when it reaches the larger body of water it spreads out and deposits the sediment. An example would be the Mississippi Delta, where the Mississippi River meets the Gulf of Mexico. A **canyon** is a deep ravine between two cliffs. It is usually formed by the erosion of flowing water over extended periods of time. A famous example of this is the Grand Canyon in Arizona. A **sand dune** is a mound of sand built by natural forces, usually wind, over time. Great Sand Dunes National Park, located in Colorado, is home to the tallest sand dunes in the United States.

Role of Water

Water plays an important role in the rock cycle through its roles in **erosion** and **weathering**: it wears down rocks; it contributes to the dissolution of rocks and minerals as acidic soil water; and it carries ions and rock fragments (sediments) to basins where they will be compressed into **sedimentary rock**. Water also plays a role in the **metamorphic processes** that occur underwater in newly-formed igneous rock at mid-ocean ridges. The presence of water (and other volatiles) is a vital component in the melting of rocky crust into magma above subduction zones.

Review Video: Igneous, Sedimentary, and Metamorphic Rocks
Visit mometrix.com/academy and enter code: 689294

Soils

Soils are formed when rock is broken down into smaller and smaller fragments by physical, chemical, and biological processes. This is called **weathering**. *Physical processes* include **erosion** and **transportation** by water and wind, freezing and thawing, and slumping due to gravity. *Chemical changes* alter the original substances present in rocks and early-stage soils. *Biological* *processes* include burrowing by animals like earthworms and rodents and penetration by plant roots. As plants and animals die and **decay**, soils become rich in dark organic matter called *humus*.

Properties of Soil

Since soil is a mixture of rock fragments and biological materials, it varies significantly. The composition of soil determines whether it will be good for plant life or not. Several properties of soil can be used to identify its composition, which can be helpful for adjusting it for suitability for plant growth.

- **Texture** refers to the size of the particles, which are classified as sand, silt, or clay, depending on the size and mixture of the particles.
- **Structure** refers to the density and arrangement of the soil particles. Soil can be compacted, making it dense and rock-like or it can be loose and easy to work with when planting.
- **Porosity** refers to how well water flows through the soil. A higher sand content usually allows water to flow through the soil more easily, whereas clay tends to hold onto water.
- **Chemistry** cannot be seen, but can be tested for the actual elements present in a sample of soil.
- **Color** of soil changes based on the types of minerals and organic matter in the soil. Redder soil may indicate that there is oxidized (rusted) iron in the soil, for instance.

Natural Resources

The term **natural resources** refers to products and energy that can be harvested from the world and used.

- **Water** is one of the most abundant resources on the Earth and is necessary for life.
- **Natural gas** and **oil** exist underground and deep in the ocean and can be used as fuel for machines.
- **Trees** can be harvested for wood and paper and other byproducts that are used in daily life.
- **Metals** can be harvested from the ground and are used in many applications, such as building materials and in electronics.
- **Sand** can be used to make glass, soaps, and electronics.
- **Sunlight** and **wind** can be harvested with solar panels and wind turbines to generate electricity.
- **Animal products** are used for food or materials in clothing and some manufacturing processes.

Renewable and Non-renewable Resources

Materials and energy on the Earth are classified as either renewable or non-renewable. The term **renewable resources** refers to resources that are not going to run out due to overuse or can be easily reclaimed once used. This includes the Sun, wind, and water. Some plants and animals grow so fast that it would be very challenging to run out and cause any form of extinction. **Non-renewable resources** include materials that take a very long time to produce, such as fossil fuels and coal. Once the Earth's population uses these materials up, it is very difficult to obtain or impossible to create more. Because renewable resources do not run out, whereas non-renewable resources do, environmentalists and scientists are always looking for new renewable resources to supply the planet with energy and for ways to reduce consumption of non-renewable resources. This reduction of consumption is known as **conservation**.

Weather

Heat energy from the Sun warms different parts of the planet in different ways at different times. As warm air rises it expands and cools. This causes moisture to condense as liquid drops or freeze as ice crystals to form clouds. When the water drops or ice crystals become too large to stay aloft, they fall as precipitation. As warm air rises it also leaves a low pressure zone behind. This causes air from high surrounding high pressure zones to rush in as wind.

Clouds

Clouds form when water vapor in the atmosphere cools to the point where it condenses out as water droplets or small particles of frozen ice crystals that we can see. Clouds can also form when more moisture is added to the air by evaporation until the air becomes saturated and cannot hold any more water. Then the water vapor will begin to condense into visible droplets.

Precipitation Falling from a Cloud

When the condensed water droplets or ice crystals forming in the cloud grow in size and become too heavy to stay aloft, they fall as rain, snowflakes, or hail.

Lightning Bolt

Lightning is a huge electric spark that can occur inside a cloud, go from one cloud to another, or go from a cloud to the ground. The turbulent rising air and rising and falling raindrops or ice crystals in a thunderstorm cause differences in electric charge in different parts of the cloud and between the bottom of the cloud and the ground. When the difference in charge is large enough, a lightning bolt will discharge which neutralizes the difference.

Thunder

As a lightning bolt travels through the air, it pushes the air aside faster than the speed of sound. This produces a shock wave of very hot air that creates a loud sonic boom, which we hear as thunder. If a person can hear thunder, he needs to get indoors quickly as possible since he could be struck by lightning.

We hear thunder later because sound travels much slower than light. Light travels so fast that it is almost instantaneous from one point to another anywhere on Earth. Sound travels much more slowly—about one mile every five seconds or so. Light would travel one mile in only about 5 millionths of a second. Therefore, the distance from a lightning flash can be determined by counting the number of seconds until the thunder it made is heard.

Tornado

A tornado is a violent rotating column of air that is in contact with both the ground and a cloud. The column is visible because the very low pressure causes water vapor to condense out as visible water droplets. Where the tornado touches the ground it usually stirs up a cloud of dirt and debris like the one in this photo. Tornadoes are the most violent storms on Earth, and the strongest spin at 300 miles per hour.

Hurricane

A **hurricane** is a very large tropical storm that forms over the open ocean and produces very strong winds and heavy rains. A **tropical storm** forms when warm water evaporates and the saturated air rises and forms a column of condensed water vapor. As the wind speed increases the pressure falls even more and a hurricane can be born. Sinking air in the center of the storm produces an **eye** (arrow) where the weather is quite calm and free of clouds.

Measuring Weather

Weather can be measured by a variety of methods. The simplest include measurement of rainfall, sunshine, pressure, humidity, temperature, and cloudiness with basic instruments such as thermometers, barometers, and rain gauges. However, the use of **radar** (which involves analysis of microwaves reflecting off of raindrops) and satellite imagery grants meteorologists a look at the big picture of weather across, for example, an entire continent. This helps them understand and make predictions about current and developing weather systems. Infrared (heat-sensing) imaging allows meteorologists to measure the temperature of clouds above ground. Using weather reports gathered from different weather stations spread over an area, meteorologists create synoptic charts. The locations and weather reports of several stations are plotted on a chart; analysis of the pressures reported from each location, as well as rainfall, cloud cover, and so on, can reveal basic weather patterns.

Water Cycle

The **water cycle** refers to the circulation of water in the Earth's hydrosphere (below the surface, on the surface, and above the surface of the Earth). This continuous process involves five physical actions.

- **Evaporation** refers to liquid water heating up and changing to into a gas, known as water vapor.
- **Transpiration** is where water inside of plants evaporates directly out of plant leaves.
- **Condensation** refers to the water vapor cooling down and beginning to turn back into a liquid form, causing clouds to form.
- **Precipitation** refers to the rain, snow, hail, or sleet that falls from clouds once the water vapor has condensed enough.

- The **storage** stage of the water cycle refers to the water being stored in the ground, trees, or bodies of water on the earth. Water is either trapped in vegetation (interception) or absorbed into the surface (infiltration). Runoff, caused by gravity, physically moves water downward into oceans or other water bodies.

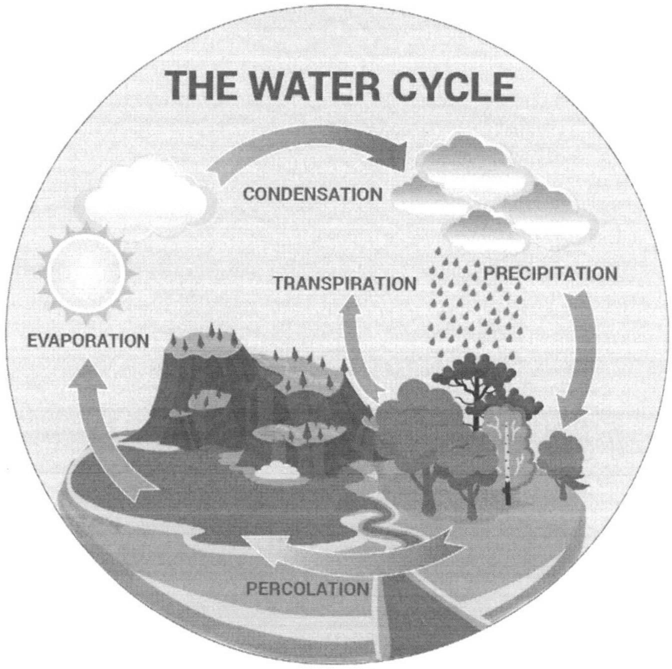

Review Video: Hydrologic Cycle
Visit mometrix.com/academy and enter code: 426578

Organisms and Environments

Producers, Consumers, and Decomposers

Producers are organisms that can make their own food. Most producers are plants. Through photosynthesis plants make sugars that provide energy. Plants only need sunlight, water, and the proper minerals and other nutrients to live, grow, and reproduce themselves. **Consumers** are organisms that eat other organisms. Consumers are animals that eat plants or other animals that eat plants. Decomposers are organisms that feed on decaying plant and animal matter. Since decomposers cannot make their own food they are classified as consumers. Fungi such as mushrooms are **decomposers** that break down the tissues and wood of living or dead plants or the bodies of dead animals.

Energy Pyramid

Energy flow through an ecosystem can be tracked through an energy pyramid. An **energy pyramid** shows how energy is transferred from one trophic level to another. **Producers** always form the base of an energy pyramid, and the consumers form successive levels above the producers. Producers only store about 1% of the solar energy they receive. Then, each successive level only uses about 10% of the energy of the previous level. That means that **primary consumers** use about 10% of the energy used by primary producers, such as grasses and trees. Next, **secondary consumers** use 10% of primary consumers' 10%, or 1% overall. This continues up for as many trophic levels as exist in a particular ecosystem.

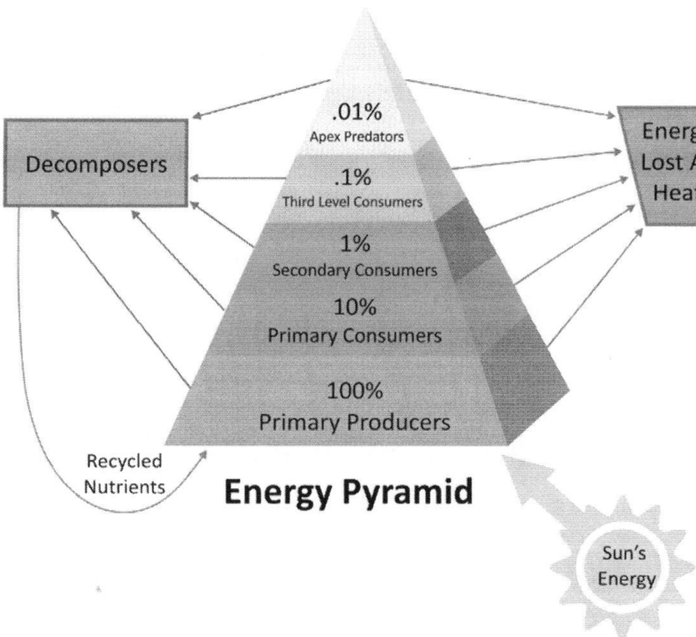

Food Web

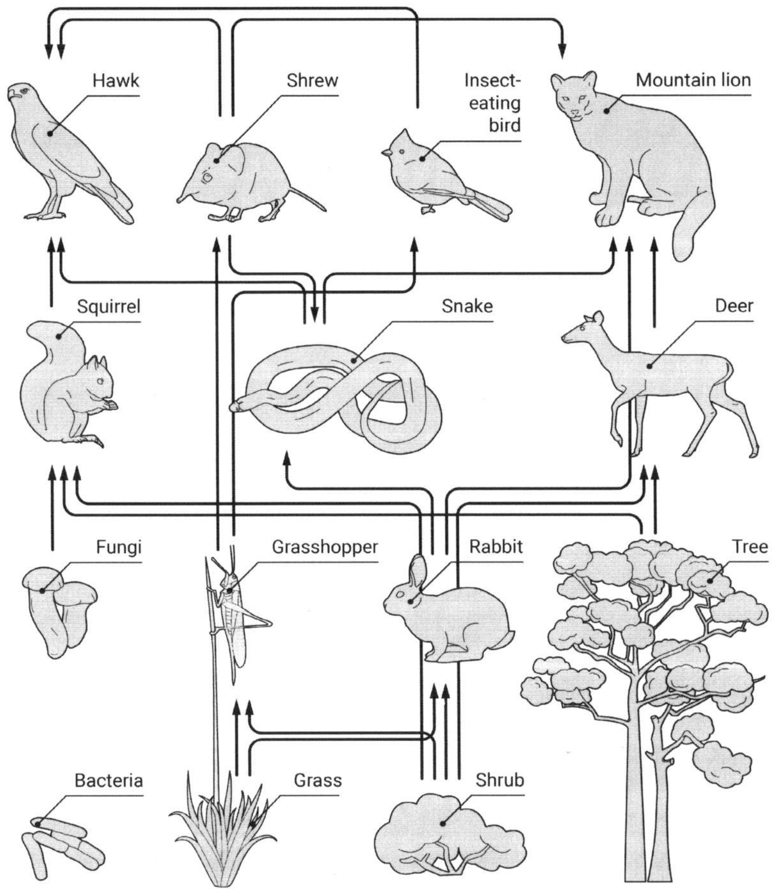

Energy flow through an ecosystem can be illustrated by a **food web**. Energy moves through the food web in the direction of the arrows. In the food web, **producers** such as grass, trees, and shrubs use energy from the Sun to produce food through photosynthesis. **Herbivores** or **primary consumers** such as squirrels, grasshoppers, and rabbits obtain energy by eating the producers. **Secondary consumers**, which are carnivores such as snakes and shrews, obtain energy by eating the primary consumers. **Tertiary consumers**, which are carnivores such as hawks and mountain lions, obtain energy by eating the secondary consumers.

Review Video: Food Webs
Visit mometrix.com/academy and enter code: 853254

Interdependence of the Food Web

Because each level of consumer is dependent on the previous level for food, the population of each level affects the other animal groups. For instance, if an ecosystem is made up of only grass, deer, and wolves, the grass are the producers, the deer eat the grass, and the wolves eat the deer. If deer are overhunted one year, the grass is given room to grow more because less of it is consumed, but the wolves will not have enough food, so the population will reduce size. Eventually, because of the abundance of grass and a reduced population of wolves, the deer may then have a surge of population. This example is an over-simplistic example, as there are usually many more producers, consumers, and predators within an ecosystem.

Populations of Animals or Plants

A population consists of all of the organisms of a certain kind in a defined area, region, or habitat. It may be all the red foxes in a given national park, all the loblolly pines in Virginia (very hard to count), all the bullfrogs in a certain pond, or even all of the boxelder bugs on a single box elder tree. In the case of rare or endangered species it may be all of the individuals still living in the wild.

Several factors operate to keep animal and plant populations under control. Predation, grazing, disease, competition for limiting resources such as food or nutrients, water, habitat and living space, hunting and breeding territory, and sunlight for plants all play important roles. Even the size of the population can influence factors such as birth rate and severity of disease outbreaks or force individuals to migrate to other less crowded areas.

Plant Species Competing with Each Other

Creosote bush is the most widespread shrub in the deserts of the American Southwest where water can be very scarce for long periods. The roots of mature creosote bushes are extremely efficient and absorb all the water in the sandy soil around them. This creates very dry zones around each plant. The seeds of other plants cannot survive long enough to germinate. Therefore, the plants tend to be spaced far apart from each other.

Food Web in a Pond

Sunlight allows green algae to photosynthesize and grow. The algae are fed upon by small animals like water fleas and copepods. In turn, these are eaten by small worms, mosquito larvae and other larval insects. These are then eaten by mosquito fish, which in turn are eaten by larger fishes like bluegills. The bluegills are preyed upon by even larger fishes like bass and by herons, egrets and raccoons (which also eat the bass). Then the animal waste and everything that dies and settles to the bottom is decomposed by bacteria and fungi.

Food Web in a Meadow

Sunlight allows grass and other plants to grow. These plants are eaten by a variety of *herbivores* like insects, rodents, and rabbits. Their seeds are consumed by various birds such as sparrows and quail. The insects are eaten by *carnivores*, including other kinds of birds, shrews, and bats. The rodents, rabbits, and some of the birds are then eaten by larger carnivores like weasels and foxes. Also, the quail, mice, rabbits and shrews are eaten by owls at night and by hawks during the day.

Animals of the Same Species Competing with Each Other

Male elk known as bulls have large antlers, which they shed and regrow each year. Like their smaller deer cousins, bull elk engage in bugling contests and ritual combat (like the photo below) to dominate other males and win all the female (cow) elk in a harem.

Different species of animals often compete for food. The spotted hyena and the African lion shown here compete for prey like zebras and wildebeest. Both hyenas and lions run in groups. A larger pack of hyenas can drive a smaller pride of lions away from prey the lions have killed. However, one lion can easily kill one or more hyenas. They rarely tolerate each other as they seem to be doing below.

Animal Migration

Many animals make a regular two-way, long-distance journey due to seasonal changes affecting the availability of food, weather or rainfall. Birds are especially noted for this, but other animals like bats, some butterflies, moths, and grasshoppers also migrate back and forth between northern winter and southern summer territories. Caribou and wildebeest also make spectacular migrations. The figure at right shows the 14,000-mile migration route of the Swainson's hawk, which spends its summers in western North America and winters in South America.

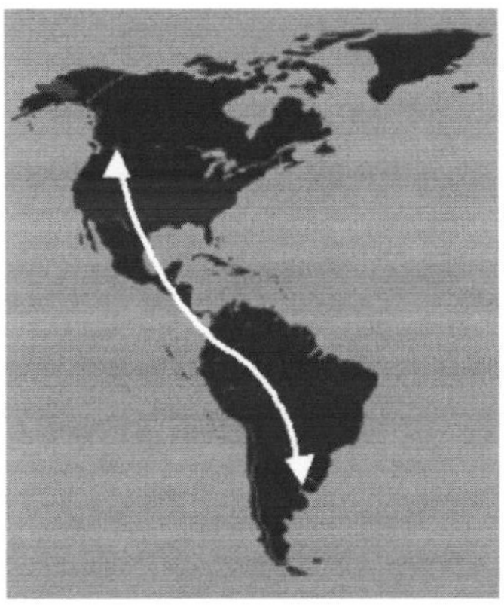

Learned Behaviors in Animals

Many behaviors in higher animals such as birds and mammals actually have to be learned. Bird songs are usually learned. Male cardinals sing slightly different songs in different areas of the country. They learn these dialects from the adult birds around them. Also, unlike the instinctive migration of spawning salmon, sandhill cranes must be taught the long migration routes they fly between their nesting and winter grounds. Likewise, most predatory mammals must learn how to hunt from their mothers.

Fastest Land Animal

The fastest animal on planet Earth is the cheetah. A cheetah can run between 70 and 75 miles per hour for almost two thirds of a mile and can go from a dead stop to 62 miles per hour in three seconds. It stalks its small antelope prey to within a short distance and then chases it down. Since the gazelle being chased in this picture can only run at 50 miles per hour, the faster cheetah has a good chance of running it down.

Animals that Mostly Come Out at Night

Nocturnal animals are active at night and sleep during the day. Nocturnal animals generally have very good senses of hearing and smell, and specially adapted eyes for seeing in the dark. Hunting or foraging for food at night is one way of avoiding competition for those resources from *diurnal* animals that are active during the day. Hawks and owls avoid competing with each other for prey in this way. Nocturnal animals also avoid the intense heat of the day in hot regions like deserts.

Hibernation

Hibernation occurs when an animal enters a state of inactivity in which its body temperature drops, and its breathing and metabolism slow down, and it goes into a deep sleep for many days, weeks, or even months. This allows animals to survive long, cold winters when food is scarce. Bears, ground squirrels and other rodents, some bats like the one shown hibernating here, and certain kinds of snakes are known to hibernate. Some animals sleep through hot summer weather or droughts. This is called *aestivation*.

Organisms and Adapted Environment

Animals and plants are adapted to live in their environments in many special ways. For example, polar bears have white fur as camouflage which helps them blend in with their icy and snowy background. This makes it easier to sneak up on the seals on which they prey. They also have thick fur and a thick layer of blubber to help keep them warm in their frigid environment.

Instinctive Behaviors

Instinctive behaviors are actions that are automatic in an animal and do not have to be taught or learned. Newly hatched sea turtles automatically crawl across the beach towards the ocean with no mother around to show them what to do. Tree squirrels automatically store acorns and nuts during the summer in order to have food in the coming winter. Also, salmon automatically return from the ocean to the freshwater river where they hatched in order to spawn.

Camouflage and Mimicry

Generally speaking, *camouflage* is when an organism blends in with its surroundings in a way that it cannot be seen as in the case of the flounder blending in with the gravel on the bottom of a lake (Fig. B). *Mimicry* is when an organism resembles something else, like the leaf insect in Fig. A. In these two examples each animal is able to avoid being seen and eaten by a predator. However, sometimes it is the predator that is camouflaged or a mimic which enables it to pounce on its unsuspecting prey.

Warning Coloration

Dangerously venomous or poisonous animals often are brightly colored to warn predators that they are best left alone. This is called aposematic coloration. The deadly venomous coral snake (Fig. A.)

has bright red, yellow and black bands that circle its body. The harmless milk snake (Fig. B) mimics the dangerous coral snake which fools predators to leave them alone, too.

Competition between Different Organisms

Animals and plants have to compete with other species for food or nutrients, water, a place to live, nesting or breeding sites, sunlight in the case of plants, and other factors in the environment that may be scarce or limiting. Also, animals and plants of the same species have to compete with each other for the same things, as well in some cases for the right to breed and reproduce.

Genetics and Heredity

Genetics is the study of biological inheritance in organisms. Animals generally reproduce with a mother and a father, which both contribute their **genetic** information to offspring. The passing along of genetic traits is also known as **heredity**. The offspring of a mother with red hair and blue eyes with a father who has brown hair and brown eyes may receive any combination of those traits. Another example may be a red fox mating with a brown fox; the offspring may have either brown fur or red fur, and a pack of siblings may have a mixture of inherited traits. This type of inheritance can also be seen in plant life, as pink and white flowered plants may breed together to produce either pink or white flowered offspring, or even special hybrids with blended colors.

Innate Behaviors

Similar to genetics, there are some behaviors that are innate, or instinctual. Many animals do not nurture their young, but instead, the newborn creatures are capable of fending for themselves. Below are some examples of innate behaviors that are not learned or taught.

- Birds migrate from North to South for the winter to protect themselves from the cold.
- Salmon swim upstream to nesting grounds.
- Some insects migrate and form cocoons to metamorphose.
- Rattlesnakes shake their rattles to warn other animals.

Learned Behaviors

Some behaviors and traits may be inherited, but many behaviors must be taught by the parents or pack to the young. Below are some examples of learned or taught behaviors.

- A wolf pack teaches the young wolves how to hunt effectively as a group.
- Some primates use sticks as tools to gather food.
- Dogs learn tricks and commands from their owners.
- Pelicans learn to hunt for fish in groups.
- Humans teach their children words and how to read.

Changes throughout the Life Cycle

Many types of plants and animals go through a process of changes throughout their lifespan. This process involves a complete change in how the plant or animal looks and acts during that life stage. In insects and in amphibians, this is called **metamorphosis**.

Tomato Plant Life Cycle

Tomato plants undergo a series of life stages, starting at the seed. The **seed** contains all of its own nutrition for the beginning stages of life. Once it is planted, it grows into a **seedling** and starts using photosynthesis to harness the energy for life and growth. When the plant is **mature**, it produces **flowers** which then produce the tomato fruit. The **fruit** contains seeds which then go on to become the next generation for this plant. The tomato plant usually dies after one year, so the next generation comes directly from the seeds of the previous generation.

Lima Bean Life Cycle

Lima beans have similar life cycles are similar to that of a tomato plan. It begins are a seed, which grows roots underground. As it grows and emerges from the soil, it becomes a seedling, which eventually becomes an adult lima bean plant. Rather than flowering, it produces leaves and pods, which contain several new seeds. These seeds are known as beans, which can be replanted or cooked for food.

Radish Life Cycle

Radishes also begin as a seed, which germinates into a sprout. The radish grows large leaves above ground while the root underground also grows large and round. When the plant grows into an adult, it flowers, producing more seeds. The large root underground is generally what most people think of as a radish, and the leaves that grow above ground are known as radish greens. Both the root and the leaves are cooked and eaten.

Frog Life Cycle

Frogs have a very distinctive life cycle. Frogs start out as eggs, which hatch into tadpoles. Tadpoles live and breathe completely in the water using gills and have no legs or arms to walk with. As the tadpole begins to mature, it grows legs and eventually becomes a young frog. The young frogs then emerge from the water and usually live on land and breathe air using lungs. Some frogs are still able to live and breathe underwater throughout their adult life. Frogs then reproduce by laying eggs in the water.

Lady Beetle and Butterfly Life Cycles

Lady Beetles, commonly called ladybugs and butterflies start their lives as eggs, which then hatch into a larva, which is most similar to a worm. In butterflies, this is called a caterpillar. The larva usually spends its life eating to build up energy for the change to its next stage. The larva eventually turns into a pupa or a chrysalis, which is a far less active stage. In this change, the larva spins a web around itself, becoming a cocoon. In this stage, the body changes form and eventually, an adult butterfly or ladybug emerges. The adult forms of both of these creatures have wings and are then able to fly and eventually produce new eggs.

Cricket Life Cycle

Crickets undergo a similar but far less dramatic lifecycle change than metamorphosing insects. They start as eggs, which hatch into **nymph** crickets, which are essentially the same as the adult form of the insect, only smaller and not capable of reproducing yet. As the nymph grows, it eventually comes into adulthood and can then mate and lay eggs.

Homology

Homology is the similarity of structures of different species based on a similar anatomy in a common evolutionary ancestor. For instance, the forelimbs of humans, dogs, birds, and whales all have the same basic pattern of the bones. Specifically, all of these organisms have a humerus, radius, and ulna. They are all modifications of the same basic evolutionary structure from a common ancestor. Tetrapods resemble the fossils of extinct transitional animal called the *Eusthenopteron*. This would seem to indicate that evolution primarily modifies preexisting structures.

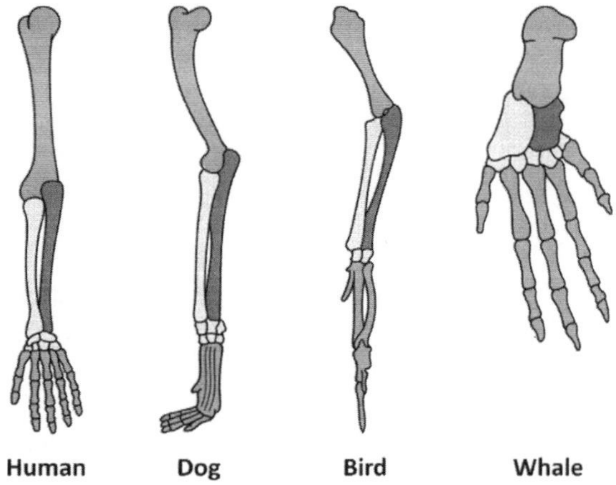

Genetics and Heredity

Genetics is the study of biological inheritance in organisms. Animals generally reproduce with a mother and a father, which both contribute their **genetic** information to offspring. The passing along of genetic traits is also known as **heredity**. The offspring of a mother with red hair and blue eyes with a father who has brown hair and brown eyes may receive any combination of those traits. Another example may be a red fox mating with a brown fox; the offspring may have either brown fur or red fur, and a pack of siblings may have a mixture of inherited traits. This type of inheritance can also be seen in plant life, as pink and white flowered plants may breed together to produce either pink or white flowered offspring, or even special hybrids with blended colors.

Modes of Reproduction

Animals can reproduce sexually or asexually. Most animals reproduce sexually. In **sexual reproduction**, males and females have different reproductive organs that produce **gametes**. Males have testes that produce sperm, and females have ovaries that produce eggs. During fertilization, a sperm cell unites with an egg cell, forming a **zygote**. Fertilization can occur internally such as in most mammals and birds or externally such as aquatic animals such as fish and frogs. The zygote undergoes cell division, which develops into an embryo and eventually develops into an adult organism. Some embryos develop in eggs such as in fish, amphibians, reptiles, and birds. Some mammals are **oviparous** meaning that they lay eggs, but most are **viviparous** meaning they have a uterus in which the embryo develops. One particular type of mammal called **marsupials** give birth to an immature fetus that finishes development in a pouch. However, there are some animals reproduce **asexually**. For example, hydras reproduce by budding, and starfish and planarians can reproduce by fragmentation and regeneration. Some fish, frogs, and insects can even reproduce by parthenogenesis, which is a type of self-reproduction without fertilization.

Effects of the Modes of Reproduction on Offspring

With **asexual reproduction**, an organism provides all of the **genes** to its offspring, making it like a **clone**, or exactly like the parent in its genetic makeup. This means that the offspring will be very similar to the parent unless there is a random mutation that causes a change. This means that the offspring will be very uniform to each other. In **sexual reproduction**, both parents provide genetic information that can be inherited, causing much more variety in the offspring from generation to generation. This more aggressive variation means that natural selection and adaptation is more likely to make a difference for the species in the long-term.

Due to mutations over long periods, genes come in alternate forms, called **alleles**, that determine how a **trait** will be represented in the offspring. Different alleles govern many different traits. Sexual reproduction makes new combinations of existing alleles. These new combinations lead to variations in physical and behavioral traits that lead to adaptation and selection, which are key components of evolution.

Mitosis

Eukaryotic cells divide into two genetically identical daughter cells in a process called mitosis. Meiosis is another form of cell division that produces haploid gametes for sexual reproduction. At the beginning of mitosis, DNA chromatin condenses into chromosomes, which replicate themselves forming two sister chromatids joined by a centromere. These chromosomes line up along an equatorial plate in the center of the cell, the centromere divides, and each of the two paired chromatids is pulled to opposites sides of the cell by microtubules attached to the centromere and the star-shaped centrosome. The cytoplasm then divides in a process called cytokinesis. At the end of mitosis, the diploid ($2n$) genome of the original cell, the entirety of the parent cell's DNA, is passed on to each daughter cell.

Meiosis

Sexual reproduction in eukaryotic organisms involves a form of cell division known as meiosis, in which a diploid ($2n$) primary germ cell gives rise to haploid (n) gametes or spores. The diploid germ cell contains two exact copies of each chromosome (known as a homologous pair) in its genome, one from each parent. As in mitosis, meiosis begins by DNA replication and the doubling of each chromosome into two sister chromatids. The homologous pairs then come together along the equatorial plate and usually exchange fragments from one chromosome to the other—known as crossing over or recombination. Thus, genetic material from the paternal and maternal chromosomes are exchanged. The reshuffled homologous pairs are pulled to opposite poles of the cell and the cell divides to produce two $2n$ daughter cells that are genetically different from the parent cell (meiosis I). A second division (meiosis II) occurs next resulting in four haploid (n) gametes or spores. When two gametes combine during fertilization, a diploid zygote is formed.

Adaptation to Environment

Organisms must be able to adapt to their environment in order to thrive or survive. Individuals must be able to recognize stimuli in their surroundings and adapt quickly. For example, an individual euglena can sense light and respond by moving toward the light. Individual organisms must also be able to adapt to changes in the environment on a larger scale. For example, plants must be able to respond to the change in the length of the day to flower at the correct time. Populations must also be able to adapt to a changing environment. Evolution by **natural selection** is the process by which populations change over many generations to become better adapted to their environment, thus surviving longer and reproducing more successfully. For example, wooly mammoths were unable to adapt to a warming climate and are now extinct, but many species of deer did adapt and are abundant today.

Natural and Artificial Selection

Natural selection and artificial selection are both mechanisms of evolution. **Natural selection** is a process of nature in which a population can change over generations. Every population has variations in individual heritable traits and organisms best suited for survival typically reproduce and pass on those genetic traits to offspring to increase the likelihood of them surviving. Typically, the more advantageous a trait is, the more common that trait becomes in a population. Natural selection brings about evolutionary **adaptations** and is responsible for biological diversity. Artificial selection is another mechanism of evolution. **Artificial selection** is a process brought about by humans. Artificial selection is the selective breeding of domesticated animals and plants such as when farmers choose animals or plants with desirable traits to reproduce. Artificial selection has led to the evolution of farm stock and crops. For example, cauliflower, broccoli, and cabbage all evolved due to artificial selection of the wild mustard plant.

Example of Natural Selection

One of the most famous examples of natural selection is that of the Galapagos Medium Ground Finch. This bird populates the Galapagos islands, a small group of islands containing birds clearly related, but with distinctive traits, such as small and large beaks, specialized to eat food available on the island it lives in.

Innate Behaviors

Similar to genetics, there are some behaviors that are innate, or instinctual. Many animals do not nurture their young, but instead, the newborn creatures are capable of fending for themselves. Below are some examples of innate behaviors that are not learned or taught.

- Birds migrate from North to South for the winter to protect themselves from the cold.
- Salmon swim upstream to nesting grounds.
- Some insects migrate and form cocoons to metamorphose.
- Rattlesnakes shake their rattles to warn other animals.

Learned Behaviors

Some behaviors and traits may be inherited, but many behaviors must be taught by the parents or pack to the young. Below are some examples of learned or taught behaviors.

- A wolf pack teaches the young wolves how to hunt effectively as a group.
- Some primates use sticks as tools to gather food.
- Dogs learn tricks and commands from their owners.
- Pelicans learn to hunt for fish in groups.
- Humans teach their children words and how to read.

Historical and Current Kingdom Systems

In 1735 Carolus Linnaeus devised a two-kingdom classification system. He placed all living things into either the *Animalia* kingdom or the *Plantae* kingdom. Fungi and algae were classified as plants. Also, Linnaeus developed the binomial nomenclature system that is still used today. In 1866, Ernst Haeckel introduced a three-kingdom classification system, adding the *Protista* kingdom to Linnaeus's animal and plant kingdoms. Bacteria were classified as protists and cyanobacteria were still classified as plants. In 1938, Herbert Copeland introduced a four-kingdom classification system in which bacteria and cyanobacteria were moved to the *Monera* kingdom. In 1969, Robert Whittaker introduced a five-kingdom system that moved fungi from the plant kingdom to the *Fungi* kingdom. Some algae were still classified as plants. In 1977, Carl Woese introduced a six-kingdom system in which in the *Monera* kingdom was replaced with the *Eubacteria* kingdom and the *Archaebacteria* kingdom.

Domain Classification System

In 1990, Carl Woese introduced his domain classification system. **Domains** are broader groupings above the kingdom level. This system consists of three domains- *Archaea*, *Bacteria*, and *Eukarya*. All eukaryotes such as plants, animals, fungi, and protists are classified in the *Eukarya* domain. The *Bacteria* and *Archaea* domains consist of prokaryotes. Organisms previously classified in the *Monera* kingdom are now classified into either the *Bacteria* or *Archaea* domain based on their ribosomal RNA structure. Members of the *Archaea* domain often live in extremely harsh environments.

Review Video: Biological Classification Systems
Visit mometrix.com/academy and enter code: 736052

Taxonomies

A **taxonomy** is a classification system that helps sort out different groups of something. A strong example of a taxonomy is the classification system for animals. The animal kingdom is often depicted as a pyramid showing different levels of the taxonomy. The lower down the pyramid, the more specific the definition. For instance, an animal's Class identifies whether it is a fish, reptile, amphibian, bird, or mammal.

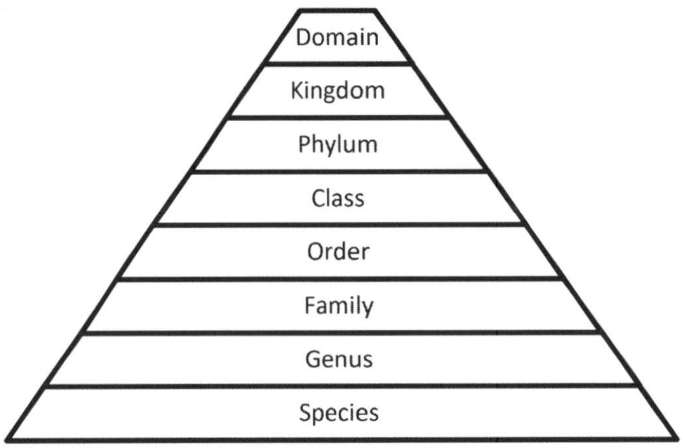

Dichotomous Keys

Dichotomous keys are an important tool for identifying and distinguishing different types of organisms or objects in a taxonomy. For instance, to identify an animal's class, we ask a series of questions that help sort out what category it belongs in. We might ask what type of animal a frog is. If you follow the dichotomous key example below, you will find that frogs do not have fur or hair, so they are not mammals. They do not have feathers, so they are not birds. Frogs have moist skin, so they are not reptiles, and they do not have scales, so they are amphibians and not fish.

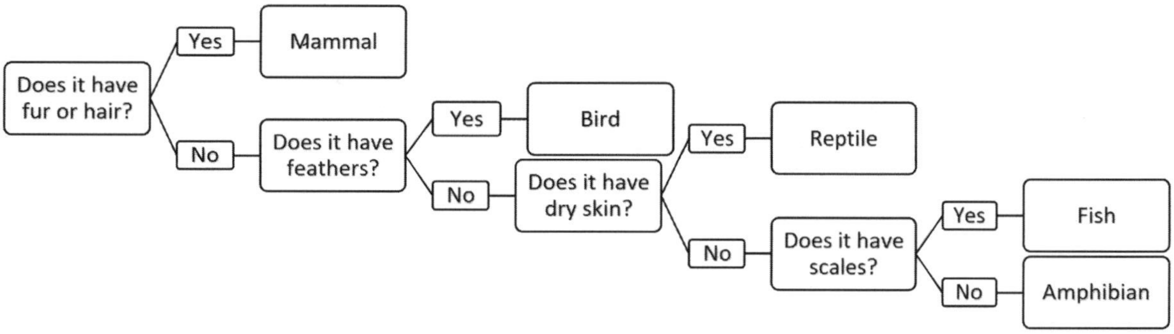

Viruses

Viruses are nonliving, infectious particles that act as parasites in living organisms. Viruses are acellular, which means that they lack cell structure. Viruses cannot reproduce outside of living cells. The structure of a virus is a nucleic acid genome, which may be either DNA or RNA, surrounded by a protective protein coat or **capsid**. In some viruses, the capsid may be surrounded by a lipid membrane or envelope. Viruses can contain up to 500 genes and have various shapes. They usually are too small to be seen without the aid of an electron microscope. Viruses can infect plants, animals, fungi, protists, and bacteria. Viruses can attack only specific types of cells that have specific receptors on their surfaces. Viruses do not divide or reproduce like living cells. Instead, they use the host cell they infect by "reprogramming" it, using the nucleic acid genome, to make more copies of the virus. The host cell usually bursts to release these copies.

Review Video: Viruses and Antiviral Drugs
Visit mometrix.com/academy and enter code: 984455

Bacteria

Bacteria are small, prokaryotic, single-celled organisms. Bacteria have a circular loop of DNA (plasmid) that is not contained within a nuclear membrane. Bacterial ribosomes are not bound to the endoplasmic reticulum, as in eukaryotes. A cell wall containing peptidoglycan surrounds the bacterial plasma membrane. Some bacteria such as pathogens are further encased in a gel-like, sticky layer called the **capsule**, which enhances their ability to cause disease. Bacteria can be autotrophs or heterotrophs. Some bacterial heterotrophs are saprophytes that function as decomposers in ecosystems. Many types of bacteria share commensal or mutualistic relationships with other organisms. Most bacteria reproduce asexually by binary fission. Two identical daughter cells are produced from one parent cell. Some bacteria can transfer genetic material to other bacteria through a process called conjugation, while some bacteria can incorporate DNA from the environment in a process called transformation.

Protists

Protists are small, eukaryotic, single-celled organisms. Although protists are small, they are much larger than prokaryotic bacteria. Protists have three general forms, which include plantlike protists, animal-like protists, and fungus-like protists. **Plantlike protists** are algae that contain chlorophyll and perform photosynthesis. Animal-like protists are **protozoa** with no cell walls that typically lack chlorophyll and are grouped by their method of locomotion, which may use flagella, cilia, or a different structure. **Fungus-like protists**, which do not have chitin in their cell walls, are generally grouped as either slime molds or water molds. Protists may be autotrophic or heterotrophic.

Autotrophic protists include many species of algae, while heterotrophic protists include parasitic, commensal, and mutualistic protozoa. Slime molds are heterotrophic fungus-like protists, which consume microorganisms. Some protists reproduce sexually, but most reproduce asexually by binary fission. Some reproduce asexually by spores while others reproduce by alternation of generations and require two hosts in their life cycle.

Fungi

Fungi are nonmotile organisms with eukaryotic cells and contain chitin in their cell walls. Most fungi are multicellular, but a few including yeast are unicellular. Fungi have multicellular filaments called **hyphae** that are grouped together into the mycelium. Fungi do not perform photosynthesis and are considered heterotrophs. Fungi can be parasitic, mutualistic or free living. Free-living fungi include mushrooms and toadstools. Parasitic fungi include fungi responsible for ringworm and athlete's foot. Mycorrhizae are mutualistic fungi that live in or near plant roots increasing the roots' surface area of absorption. Almost all fungi reproduce asexually by spores, but most fungi also have a sexual phase in the production of spores. Some fungi reproduce by budding or fragmentation.

> **Review Video: Feeding Among Heterotrophs**
> Visit mometrix.com/academy and enter code: 836017

Plants

Plants are multicellular organisms with eukaryotic cells containing cellulose in their cell walls. Plant cells have chlorophyll and perform photosynthesis. Plants can be vascular or nonvascular. **Vascular plants** have true leaves, stems, and roots that contain xylem and phloem. **Nonvascular plants** lack true leaves, stems and roots and do not have any true vascular tissue but instead rely on diffusion and osmosis to transport most of materials or resources needed to survive. Almost all plants are autotrophic, relying on photosynthesis for food. A small number do not have chlorophyll and are parasitic, but these are extremely rare. Plants can reproduce sexually or asexually. Many plants reproduce by seeds produced in the fruits of the plants, while some plants reproduce by seeds on cones. One type of plant, ferns, reproduce by a different system that utilizes spores. Some plants can even reproduce asexually by vegetative reproduction.

> **Review Video: Kingdom Plantae**
> Visit mometrix.com/academy and enter code: 710084

Organizational Hierarchy within Multicellular Organisms

Cells are the smallest living units of organisms. Tissues are groups of cells that work together to perform a specific function. Organs are groups of tissues that work together to perform a specific function. Organ systems are groups of organs that work together to perform a specific function. An organism is an individual that contains several body systems.

Cells

Cells are the basic structural units of all living things. Cells are composed of various molecules including proteins, carbohydrates, lipids, and nucleic acids. All animal cells are eukaryotic and have a nucleus, cytoplasm, and a cell membrane. Organelles include mitochondria, ribosomes, endoplasmic reticulum, Golgi apparatuses, and vacuoles. Specialized cells are numerous, including but not limited to, various muscle cells, nerve cells, epithelial cells, bone cells, blood cells, and cartilage cells. Cells are grouped to together in tissues to perform specific functions.

Tissues

Tissues are groups of cells that work together to perform a specific function. Tissues can be grouped into four broad categories: muscle tissue, connective tissue, nerve tissue, and epithelial tissue. Muscle tissue is involved in body movement. **Muscle tissues** can be composed of skeletal muscle cells, cardiac muscle cells, or smooth muscle cells. Skeletal muscles include the muscles commonly called biceps, triceps, hamstrings, and quadriceps. Cardiac muscle tissue is found only in the heart. Smooth muscle tissue provides tension in the blood vessels, controls pupil dilation, and aids in peristalsis. **Connective tissues** include bone tissue, cartilage, tendons, ligaments, fat, blood, and lymph. **Nerve tissue** is located in the brain, spinal cord, and nerves. **Epithelial tissue** makes up the layers of the skin and various membranes. Tissues are grouped together as organs to perform specific functions.

Organs and Organ Systems

Organs are groups of tissues that work together to perform specific functions. **Organ systems** are groups of organs that work together to perform specific functions. Complex animals have several organs that are grouped together in multiple systems. In mammals, there are 11 major organ systems: integumentary system, respiratory system, cardiovascular system, endocrine system, nervous system, immune system, digestive system, excretory system, muscular system, skeletal system, and reproductive system.

Cardiovascular System

The main functions of the **cardiovascular system** are gas exchange, the delivery of nutrients and hormones, and waste removal. The cardiovascular system consists primarily of the heart, blood, and blood vessels. The **heart** is a pump that pushes blood through the arteries. **Arteries** are blood vessels that carry blood away from the heart, and **veins** are blood vessels that carry blood back to the heart. The exchange of materials between blood and cells occur in the **capillaries**, which are the smallest of the blood vessels. All vertebrates and a few invertebrates including annelids, squids, and octopuses have a **closed circulatory system**, in which blood is contained in vessels and does not freely fill body cavities. Mammals, birds and crocodilians have a four-chambered heart. Most amphibians and reptiles have a three-chambered heart. Fish have only a two-chambered heart. Arthropods and most mollusks have open circulatory systems, where blood is pumped into an open cavity. Many invertebrates do not have a cardiovascular system. For example, echinoderms have a water vascular system.

Review Video: Cardiovascular System
Visit mometrix.com/academy and enter code: 376581

Review Video: Electrical Conduction System of the Heart
Visit mometrix.com/academy and enter code: 624557

Review Video: Heart Anatomy and Physiology
Visit mometrix.com/academy and enter code: 569724

Respiratory System

The function of the **respiratory system** is to move air in and out of the body in order to facilitate the exchange of oxygen and carbon dioxide. The respiratory system consists of the nasal passages, pharynx, larynx, trachea, bronchial tubes, lungs, and diaphragm. **Bronchial tubes** branch into **bronchioles**, which end in clusters of alveoli. The **alveoli** are tiny sacs inside the lungs where gas exchange takes place. When the **diaphragm** contracts, the volume of the chest increases, which reduces the pressure in the **lungs**. Then, air is inhaled through the nose or mouth and passes through the pharynx, larynx, trachea, and bronchial tubes into the lungs. When the diaphragm relaxes, the volume in the chest cavity decreases, forcing the air out of the lungs.

> **Review Video: Respiratory System**
> Visit mometrix.com/academy and enter code: 783075
>
> **Review Video: What is the Pulmonary Circuit**
> Visit mometrix.com/academy and enter code: 955608

Reproductive System

The main function of the **reproductive system** is to propagate the species. Most animals reproduce sexually at some point in their life cycle. Typically, this involves the union of a sperm and egg to produce a zygote. In complex animals, the female reproductive system includes one or more ovaries, which produce the egg cell. The male reproductive system includes one or more testes, which produce the sperm.

> **Review Video: Reproductive Systems**
> Visit mometrix.com/academy and enter code: 505450

Internal and External Fertilization

Eggs may be fertilized internally or externally. In **internal fertilization** in mammals, the sperm unites with the egg in the oviduct. In mammals, the zygote begins to divide, and the blastula implants in the uterus. Another step in internal fertilization for birds includes albumen, membranes, and egg shell develops after the egg is fertilized. Reptiles lay amniotic eggs covered by a leathery shell. Amphibians and most fish fertilize eggs **externally**, where both eggs and sperm are released into the water. However, there are some fish that give birth to live young.

Invertebrates

Most invertebrates reproduce sexually. Invertebrates may have separate sexes or be **hermaphroditic**, in which the organisms produce sperm and eggs either at the same time or separately at some time in their life cycle. Many invertebrates such as insects also have complex reproductive systems. Some invertebrates reproduce asexually by budding, fragmentation, or parthenogenesis.

Digestive System

The main function of the **digestive system** is to process the food that is consumed by the animal. This includes mechanical and chemical processing. Depending on the animal, **mechanical processes**, or the physical process of breaking food into smaller pieces, can happen in various ways. Mammals have teeth to chew their food, while many animals such as birds, earthworms, crocodilians, and crustaceans have a gizzard or gizzard-like organ that grinds the food. **Chemical digestion** includes breaking food into simpler nutrients that the body can use for specific processes. While chewing saliva is secreted, which contains enzymes to begin the breakdown of starches. Many animals such as mammals, birds, reptiles, amphibians, and fish have a stomach that stores and absorbs food. Gastric juice containing enzymes and hydrochloric acid is mixed with the food. The intestine or intestines absorb nutrients and reabsorb water from the undigested material. Many animals have a liver, gallbladder, and pancreas, which aid in digestion of proteins and fats. Undigested wasted are eliminated from the body through an anus or cloaca.

> **Review Video: Gastrointestinal System**
> Visit mometrix.com/academy and enter code: 378740

Excretory System

All animals have some type of **excretory system** that has the main function of metabolizing food and eliminating metabolic wastes. In complex animals such as mammals, the excretory system consists of the kidneys, ureters, urinary bladder, and urethra. Urea and other toxic wastes must be eliminated from the body. The kidneys constantly filter the blood and facilitate nutrient reabsorption and waste secretion. Urine passes from the kidneys through the ureters to the urinary bladder where it is stored before it is expelled from the body through the urethra.

Kidneys

The **kidneys** are involved in blood filtration, pH balance, and the reabsorption of nutrients to maintain proper blood volume and ion balance. The **nephron** is the working unit of the kidney. The parts of the nephron include the glomerulus, Bowman's capsule, and loop of Henle. Filtration takes place in the nephron's **glomerulus.** Water and dissolved materials such as glucose and amino acids pass on into the Bowman's capsule. Depending on concentration gradients, water and dissolved materials can pass back into the blood primarily through the proximal convoluted tubule. Reabsorption and water removal occurs in the **loop of Henle** and the conducting duct. Urine and other nitrogenous wastes pass from the kidneys to the bladders and are expelled.

Review Video: Urinary System
Visit mometrix.com/academy and enter code: 601053

Nervous System

All animals except sponges have a nervous system. The main function of the **nervous system** is to coordinate the activities of the body. The nervous system consists of the brain, spinal cord, peripheral nerves, and sense organs. **Sense organs** such as the ears, eyes, nose, taste buds, and pressure receptors receive stimuli from the environment and relay that information through nerves and the spinal cord to the brain where the information is processed. The **brain** sends signals through the spinal cord and peripheral nerves to the organs and muscles. The **autonomic nervous system** controls all routine body functions by the sympathetic and parasympathetic divisions. Reflexes, which are also part of the nervous system, may involve only a few nerve cells and bypass the brain when an immediate response is necessary.

Review Video: Autonomic Nervous System
Visit mometrix.com/academy and enter code: 598501

Endocrine System

The **endocrine system** consists of several ductless glands, which secrete hormones directly into the bloodstream. The **pituitary gland** is the master gland, which controls the functions of the other glands. The pituitary gland regulates skeletal growth and the development of the reproductive organs. The pineal gland regulates sleep cycles. The **thyroid gland** regulates metabolism and helps regulate the calcium level in the blood. The parathyroid glands also help regulate the blood calcium level. The **adrenal glands** secrete the emergency hormone epinephrine, stimulate body repairs, and regulate sodium and potassium levels in the blood. The **islets of Langerhans** located in the pancreas secrete insulin and glucagon to regulate the blood sugar level. In females, ovaries produce estrogen, which stimulates sexual development, and progesterone, which functions during pregnancy. In males, the testes secrete testosterone, which stimulates sexual development and sperm production.

Review Video: Endocrine System
Visit mometrix.com/academy and enter code: 678939

Immune System

The **immune system** in animals defends the body against infection and disease. The immune system can be divided into two broad categories: innate immunity and adaptive immunity. **Innate immunity** includes the skin and mucous membranes, which provide a physical barrier to prevent pathogens from entering the body. Special chemicals including enzymes and proteins in mucus, tears, sweat, and stomach juices destroy pathogens. Numerous white blood cells such as neutrophils and macrophages protect the body from invading pathogens. **Adaptive immunity** involves the body responding to a specific antigen. Typically, B-lymphocytes or B cells produce antibodies against a specific antigen, and T-lymphocytes or T-cells take special roles as helpers, regulators, or killers. Some T-cells function as memory cells.

Review Video: Immune System
Visit mometrix.com/academy and enter code: 622899

Integumentary System

This includes skin, hair, nails, sense receptors, sweat glands, and oil glands. The **skin** is a sense organ, provides an exterior barrier against disease, regulates body temperature through perspiration, manufactures chemicals and hormones, and provides a place for nerves from the nervous system and parts of the circulation system to travel through. Skin has three layers: epidermis, dermis, and subcutaneous. The **epidermis** is the thin, outermost, waterproof layer. The **dermis** has the sweat glands, oil glands, and hair follicles. The **subcutaneous layer** has connective tissue. Also, this layer has **adipose** (i.e., fat) tissue, nerves, arteries, and veins.

Review Video: Integumentary System
Visit mometrix.com/academy and enter code: 655980

Lymphatic System

The **lymphatic system** is connected to the cardiovascular system through a network of capillaries. The lymphatic system filters out organisms that cause disease, controls the production of disease-fighting antibodies, and produces white blood cells. The lymphatic system also prevents body tissues from swelling by draining fluids from them. Two of the most important areas in this system are the right lymphatic duct and the thoracic duct. The **right lymphatic duct** moves the immunity-bolstering lymph fluid through the top half of the body, while the **thoracic duct** moves lymph throughout the lower half. The spleen, thymus, and lymph nodes all generate and store the chemicals which form lymph and which are essential to protecting the body from disease.

Skeletal System

The skeletal system serves many functions including providing structural support, providing movement, providing protection, producing blood cells, and storing substances such as fat and minerals. The **axial skeleton** transfers the weight from the upper body to the lower appendages. Bones provide attachment points for muscles. The cranium protects the brain. The vertebrae protect the spinal cord. The rib cage protects the heart and lungs. The pelvis protects the reproductive organs. **Joints** including hinge joints, ball-and-socket joints, pivot joints, ellipsoid joints, gliding joints, and saddle joints. The **red marrow** manufactures red and white blood cells. All bone marrow is red at birth, but adults have approximately one-half red bone marrow and one-half yellow bone marrow. Yellow bone marrow stores fat.

Organizational Hierarchy within Multicellular Organisms

Cells are the smallest living units of organisms. Tissues are groups of cells that work together to perform a specific function. Organs are groups of tissues that work together to perform a specific function. Organ systems are groups of organs that work together to perform a specific function. An organism is an individual that contains several body systems.

Cells

Cells are the basic structural units of all living things. Cells are composed of various molecules including proteins, carbohydrates, lipids, and nucleic acids. All animal cells are eukaryotic and have a nucleus, cytoplasm, and a cell membrane. Organelles include mitochondria, ribosomes, endoplasmic reticulum, Golgi apparatuses, and vacuoles. Specialized cells are numerous, including but not limited to, various muscle cells, nerve cells, epithelial cells, bone cells, blood cells, and cartilage cells. Cells are grouped to together in tissues to perform specific functions.

Tissues

Tissues are groups of cells that work together to perform a specific function. Tissues can be grouped into four broad categories: muscle tissue, connective tissue, nerve tissue, and epithelial tissue. Muscle tissue is involved in body movement. **Muscle tissues** can be composed of skeletal muscle cells, cardiac muscle cells, or smooth muscle cells. Skeletal muscles include the muscles commonly called biceps, triceps, hamstrings, and quadriceps. Cardiac muscle tissue is found only in the heart. Smooth muscle tissue provides tension in the blood vessels, controls pupil dilation, and aids in peristalsis. **Connective tissues** include bone tissue, cartilage, tendons, ligaments, fat, blood, and lymph. **Nerve tissue** is located in the brain, spinal cord, and nerves. **Epithelial tissue** makes up the layers of the skin and various membranes. Tissues are grouped together as organs to perform specific functions.

Organs and Organ Systems

Organs are groups of tissues that work together to perform specific functions. **Organ systems** are groups of organs that work together to perform specific functions. Complex animals have several organs that are grouped together in multiple systems. In mammals, there are 11 major organ systems: integumentary system, respiratory system, cardiovascular system, endocrine system, nervous system, immune system, digestive system, excretory system, muscular system, skeletal system, and reproductive system.

Prokaryotes and Eukaryotes

Sizes and Metabolism

Cells of the domains of Bacteria and Archaea are **prokaryotes**. Bacteria cells and Archaea cells are much smaller than cells of eukaryotes. Prokaryote cells are usually only 1 to 2 micrometers in diameter, but eukaryotic cells are usually at least 10 times and possibly 100 times larger than prokaryotic cells. Eukaryotic cells are usually 10 to 100 micrometers in diameter. Most prokaryotes are unicellular organisms, although some prokaryotes live in colonies. Because of their large surface-area-to-volume ratios, prokaryotes have a very high metabolic rate. **Eukaryotic cells** are much larger than prokaryotic cells. Due to their larger sizes, they have a much smaller surface-area-to-volume ratio and consequently have much lower metabolic rates.

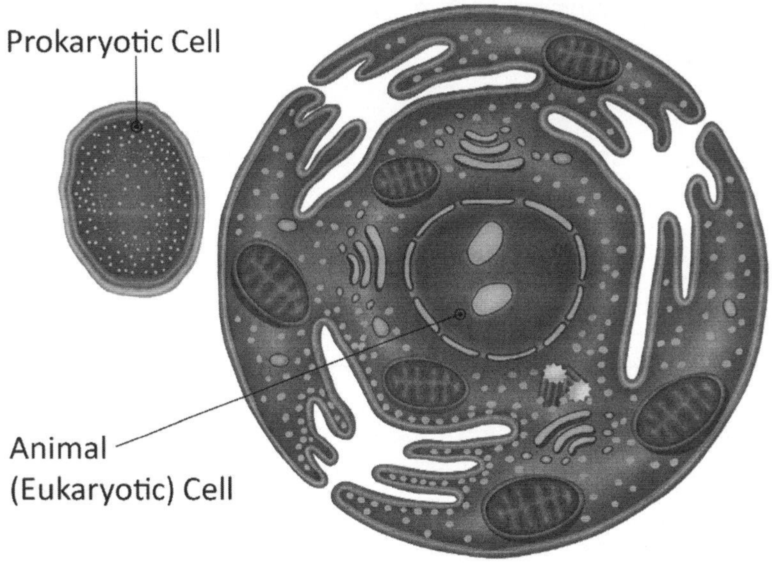

Review Video: Eukaryotic and Prokaryotic Cells
Visit mometrix.com/academy and enter code: 231438

Review Video: Cell Structure
Visit mometrix.com/academy and enter code: 591293

Membrane-Bound Organelles

Prokaryotic cells are much simpler than eukaryotic cells. Prokaryote cells do not have a nucleus due to their small size and their DNA is located in the center of the cell in a region referred to as a **nucleoid**. Eukaryote cells have a **nucleus** bound by a double membrane. Eukaryotic cells typically have hundreds or thousands of additional **membrane-bound organelles** that are independent of the cell membrane. Prokaryotic cells do not have any membrane-bound organelles that are independent of the cell membrane. Once again, this is probably due to the much larger size of the eukaryotic cells. The organelles of eukaryotes give them much higher levels of intracellular division than is possible in prokaryotic cells.

Cell Walls

Not all cells have cell walls, but most prokaryotes have cell walls. The cell walls of organisms from the domain Bacteria differ from the cell walls of the organisms from the domain Archaea. Some eukaryotes, such as some fungi, some algae, and plants, have cell walls that differ from the cell walls of the Bacteria and Archaea domains. The main difference between the cell walls of different domains or kingdoms is the composition of the cell walls. For example, most bacteria have cell walls outside of the plasma membrane that contains the molecule peptidoglycan. **Peptidoglycan** is a large polymer of amino acids and sugars. The peptidoglycan helps maintain the strength of the cell wall. Some of the Archaea cells have cell walls containing the molecule pseudopeptidoglycan, which differs in chemical structure from the peptidoglycan but basically provides the same strength to the cell wall. Some fungi cell walls contain **chitin**. The cell walls of diatoms, a type of yellow algae, contain silica. Plant cell walls contain cellulose, and woody plants are further strengthened by lignin. Some algae also contain lignin. Animal cells do not have cell walls.

CHROMOSOME STRUCTURE

Prokaryote cells have DNA arranged in a **circular structure** that should not be referred to as a chromosome. Due to the small size of a prokaryote cell, the DNA material is simply located near the center of the cell in a region called the nucleoid. A prokaryotic cell may also contain tiny rings of DNA called plasmids. Prokaryote cells lack histone proteins, and therefore the DNA is not actually packaged into chromosomes. Prokaryotes reproduce by binary fission, while eukaryotes reproduce by mitosis with the help of **linear chromosomes** and histone proteins. During mitosis, the chromatin is tightly wound on the histone proteins and packaged as a chromosome. The DNA in a eukaryotic cell is located in the membrane-bound nucleus.

> **Review Video: Chromosomes**
> Visit mometrix.com/academy and enter code: 132083

CELLS AND ORGANELLES OF PLANT CELLS AND ANIMAL CELLS

Plant cells and animal cells both have a nucleus, cytoplasm, cell membrane, ribosomes, mitochondria, endoplasmic reticulum, Golgi apparatus, and vacuoles. Plant cells have only one or two extremely large vacuoles. Animal cells typically have several small vacuoles. Plant cells have chloroplasts for photosynthesis and use this process to produce their own food, distinguishing plants as **autotrophs**. Animal cells do not have chloroplasts and therefore cannot use photosynthesis to produce their own food. Instead animal cells rely on other sources for food, which classifies them as **heterotrophs**. Animal cells have centrioles, which are used to help organize microtubules and in in cell division, but only some plant cells have centrioles. Additionally, plant cells have a rectangular and more rigid shape due to the cell wall, while animal cells have more of a circular shape because they lack a cell wall.

Review Video: Difference Between Plant and Animal Cells
Visit mometrix.com/academy and enter code: 115568

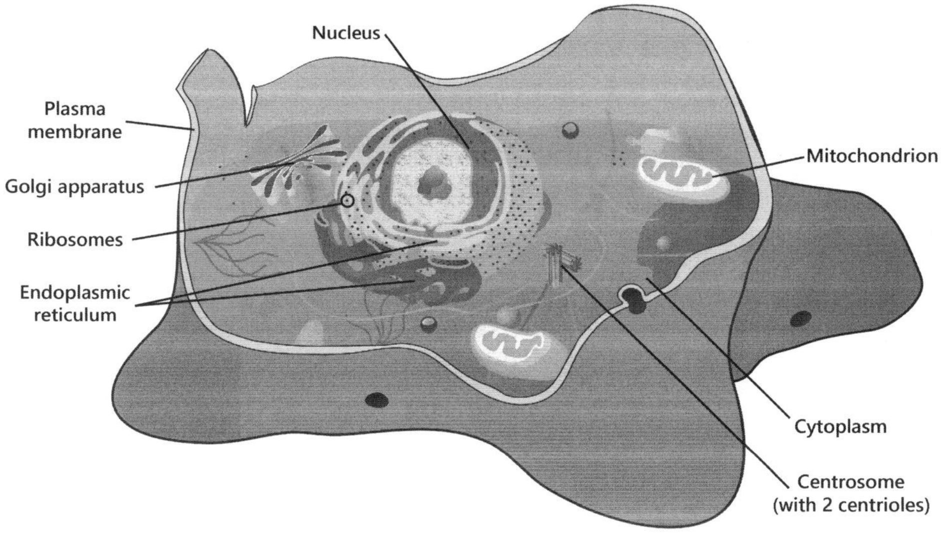

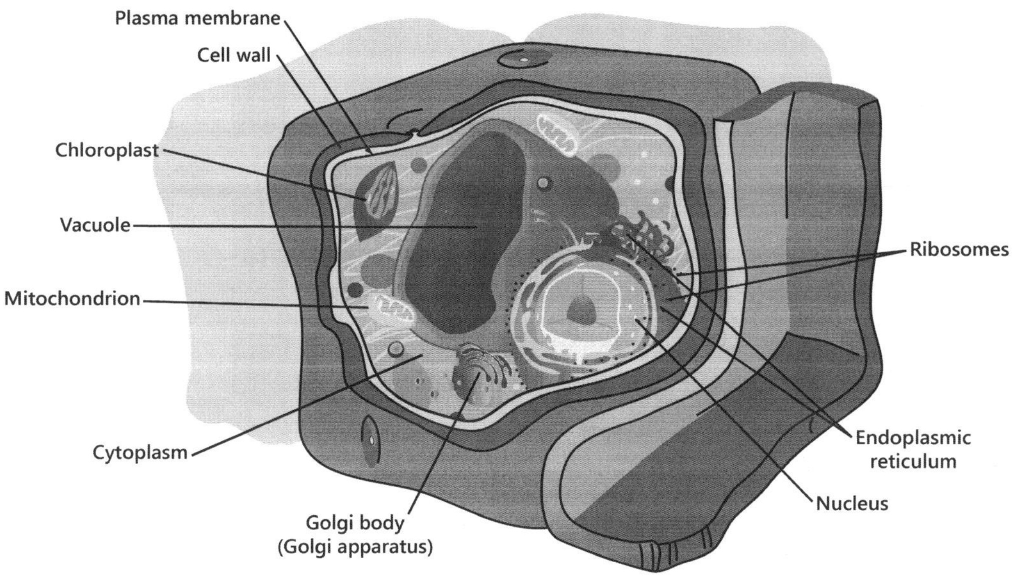

Cell Membranes

The **cell membrane**, also referred to as the plasma membrane, is a thin semipermeable membrane of lipids and proteins. The cell membrane isolates the cell from its external environment while still enabling the cell to communicate with that outside environment. It consists of a phospholipid bilayer, or double layer, with the hydrophilic ("water-loving") ends of the outer layer facing the external environment, the inner layer facing the inside of the cell, and the hydrophobic ("water-fearing") ends facing each other. Cholesterol in the cell membrane adds stiffness and flexibility. Glycolipids help the cell to recognize other cells of the organisms. The proteins in the cell membrane help give the cells shape. Special proteins help the cell communicate with its external environment, while other proteins transport molecules across the cell membrane.

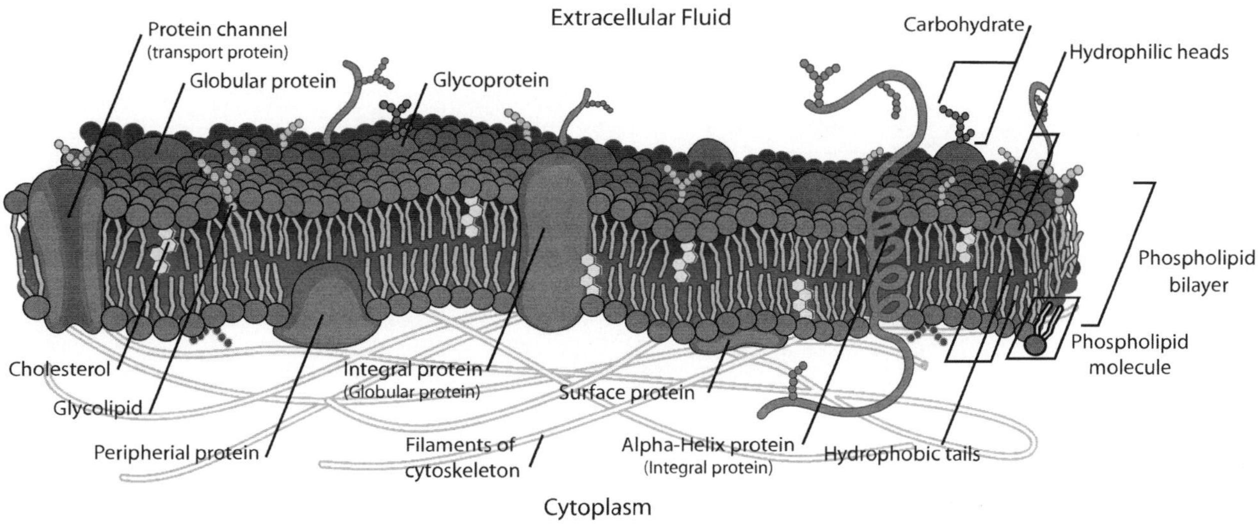

Review Video: Function of the Plasma Membrane
Visit mometrix.com/academy and enter code: 943095

Nucleus

Typically, a eukaryote has only one nucleus that takes up approximately 10% of the volume of the cell. Components of the nucleus include the nuclear envelope, nucleoplasm, chromatin, and nucleolus. The **nuclear envelope** is a double-layered membrane with the outer layer connected to the endoplasmic reticulum. The nucleus can communicate with the rest of the cell through several nuclear pores. The chromatin consists of deoxyribonucleic acid (DNA) and histones that are packaged into chromosomes during mitosis. The **nucleolus**, which is the dense central portion of the nucleus, produced and assembles ribosomes with the help of ribosomal RNA and proteins.

Functions of the nucleus include the storage of genetic material, production of ribosomes, and transcription of ribonucleic acid (RNA).

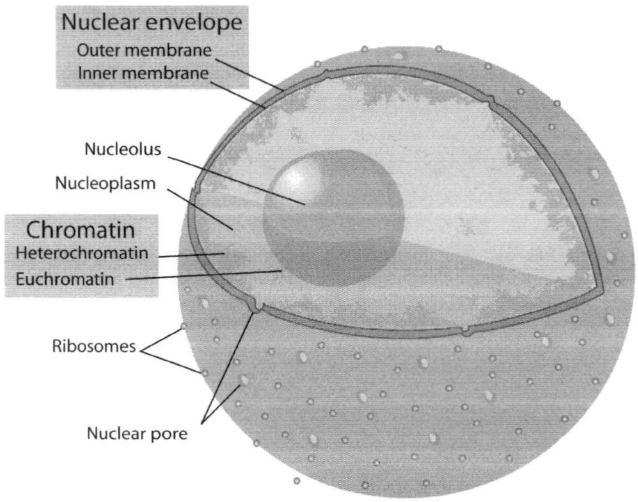

Review Video: Nucleic Acids
Visit mometrix.com/academy and enter code: 503931

Chloroplasts

Chloroplasts are large organelles that are enclosed in a double membrane. Just as cells contain a fluid called cytoplasm, chloroplasts contain a fluid called the **stroma**. Within the stroma, there are discs called **thylakoids**, which are arranged in stacks called grana (singular: granum). The thylakoids have chlorophyll molecules on their surfaces. **Stromal lamellae** separate the thylakoid stacks. Chloroplasts perform photosynthesis and make food (in the form of sugars) for the plant. The light reaction stage of photosynthesis occurs in the grana, and the dark reaction stage of photosynthesis occurs in the stroma. Sugars are formed in the stroma. Chloroplasts have their own DNA and can reproduce by fission independently.

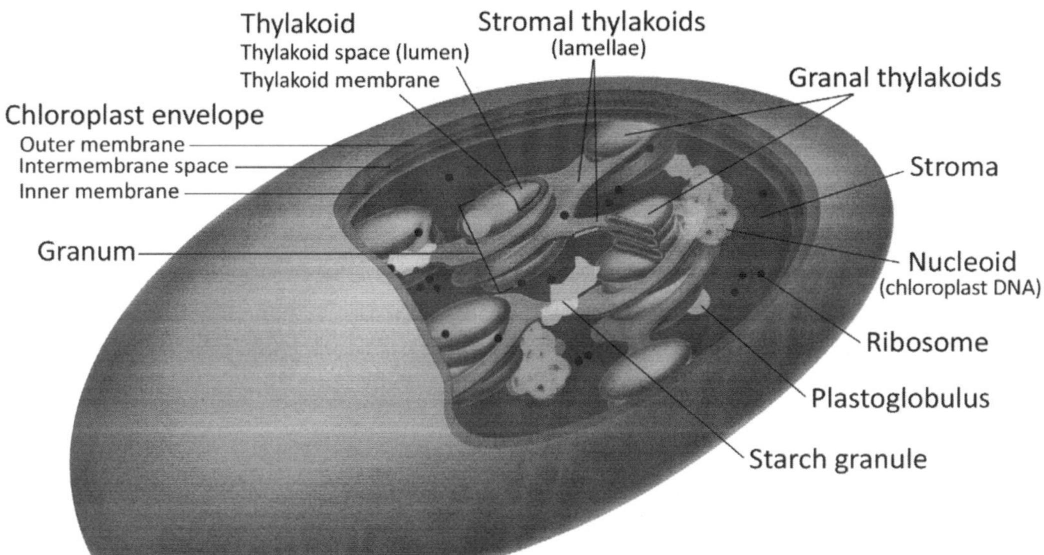

Plastids

Plastids are major organelles found in plants and algae that are used to synthesize and store food. Because plastids can differentiate, there are many forms of plastids. Specialized plastids can store pigments, starches, fats, or proteins. Two examples of plastids are amyloplasts and chloroplasts. **Amyloplasts** are the plastids that store the starch formed from long chains of glucose produced during photosynthesis. Amyloplasts synthesize and store the starch granules through the polymerization of glucose. When needed, amyloplasts also convert these starch granules back into sugar. Fruits and potato tubers have large numbers of amyloplasts. **Chloroplasts** can synthesize and store starch. Interestingly, amyloplasts can redifferentiate and transform into chloroplasts.

Mitochondria

Mitochondria break down sugar molecules and produce energy in the form of molecules of adenosine triphosphate (ATP). Both plant and animal cells contain mitochondria. Mitochondria are enclosed in a bilayer semi-membrane of phospholipids and proteins. The intermembrane space is the space between the two layers. The **outer membrane** has proteins called porins, which allow small molecules through. The **inner membrane** contains proteins that aid in the synthesis of ATP. The matrix consists of enzymes that help synthesize ATP. Mitochondria have their own DNA and can reproduce by fission independently. Mitochondria also help to maintain calcium concentrations, form blood components and hormones, and are involved in activating cell death pathways.

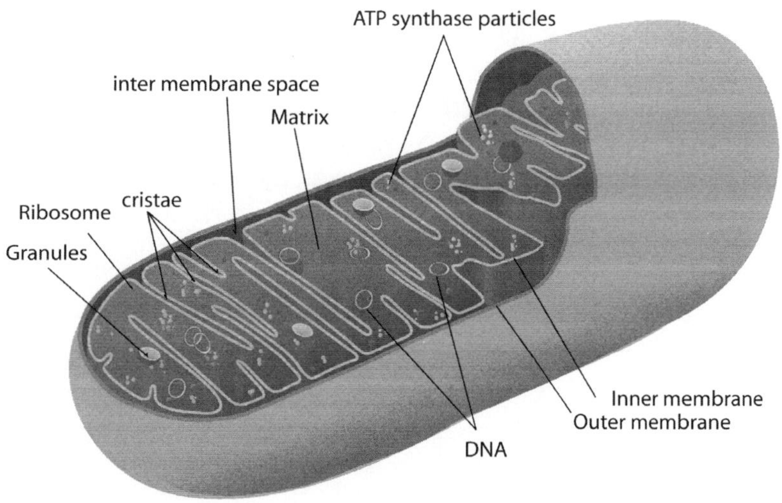

Review Video: Mitochondria
Visit mometrix.com/academy and enter code: 444287

Ribosomes

A **ribosome** consists of RNA and proteins. The RNA component of the ribosome is known as ribosomal RNA (rRNA). Ribosomes consist of two subunits, a large subunit and a small subunit. Few ribosomes are free in the cell. Most of the ribosomes in the cell are embedded in the rough endoplasmic reticulum located near the nucleus. Ribosomes are protein factories and translate the code of DNA into proteins by assembling long chains of amino acids. **Messenger RNA** (mRNA) is used by the ribosome to generate a specific protein sequence, while **transfer RNA** (tRNA) collects the needed amino acids and delivers them to the ribosome.

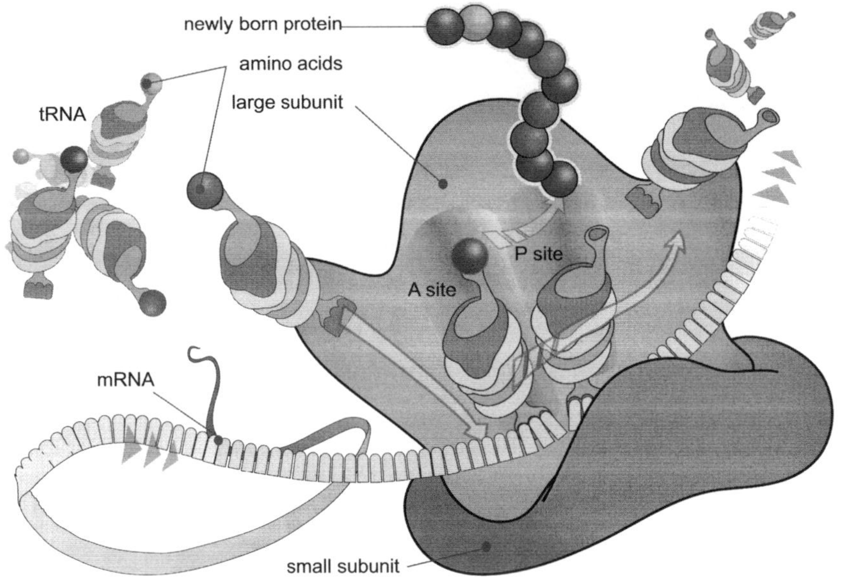

Golgi Apparatus

The **Golgi apparatus**, also called the Golgi body or Golgi complex, is a stack of flattened membranes called **cisternae** that package, ship, and distribute macromolecules such as carbohydrates, proteins, and lipids in shipping containers called **vesicles**. It also helps modify proteins and lipids before they are shipped. Most Golgi apparatuses have six to eight cisternae. Each Golgi apparatus has four regions: the cis region, the endo region, the medial region, and the trans region. Transfer vesicles from the rough endoplasmic reticulum (ER) enter at the cis region, and secretory vesicles leave the Golgi apparatus from the trans region.

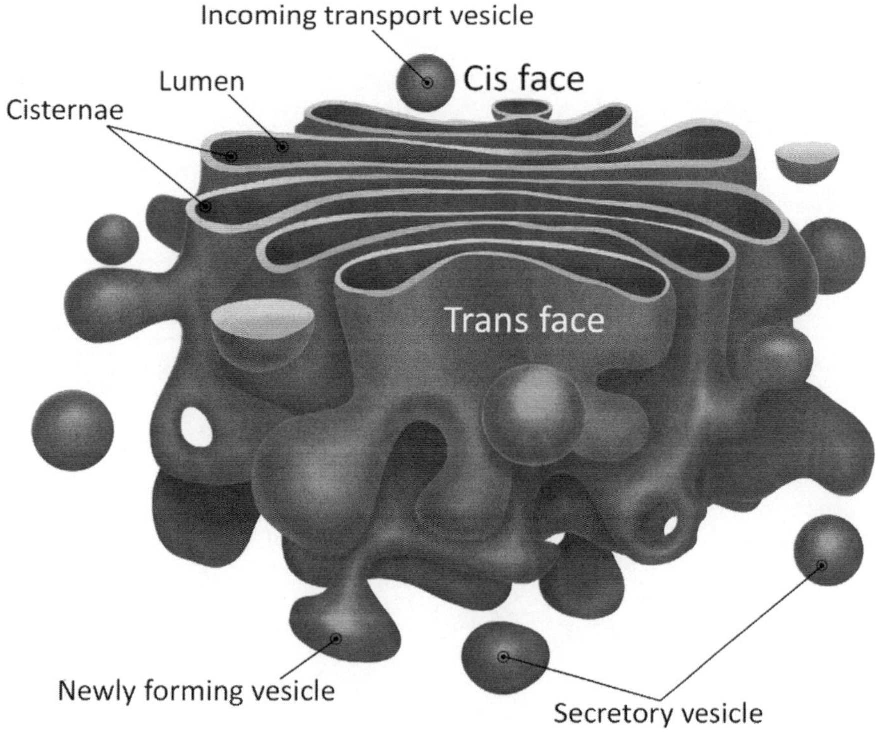

Cytoskeleton

The **cytoskeleton** is a scaffolding system located in the cytoplasm. The cytoskeleton consists of elongated organelles made of proteins called microtubules, microfilaments, and intermediate filaments. These organelles provide shape, support, and the ability to move. These structures also assist in moving the chromosomes during mitosis. Microtubules and microfilaments help transport materials throughout the cell and are the major components in cilia and flagella.

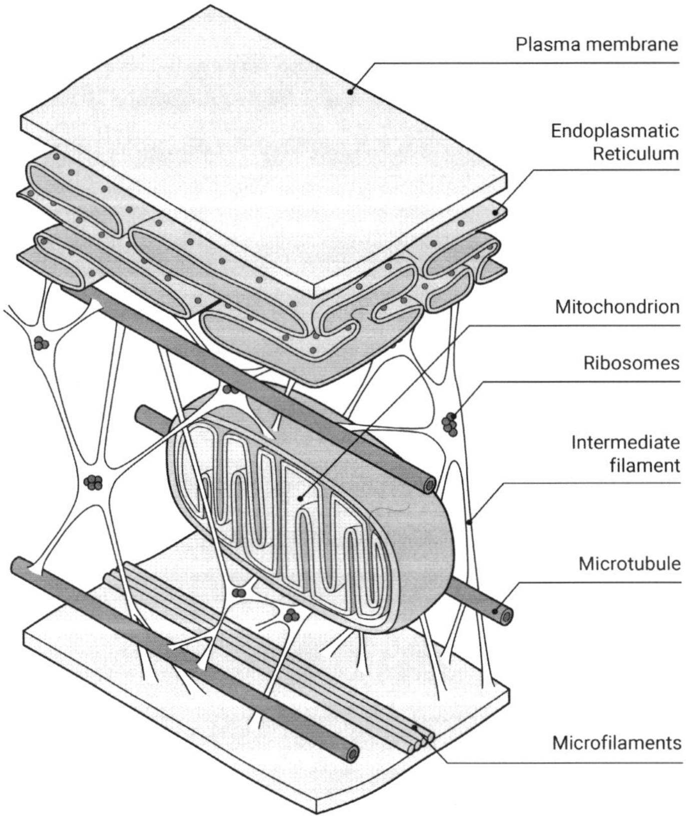

Practice Test #1

1. Weather forecasters will sometimes use the phrase "the mercury will rise" for a forecasted hot day. Why does mercury rise?

a. Molecules within the thermometer expand because of the hotter temperature. As they expand, they move up the thermometer.
b. The neck of the thermometer becomes skinnier, making the mercury rise.
c. Molecules within the thermometer shrink as the temperature gets hotter, and as they do so, move up the thermometer.
d. The phrase has nothing to do with the outside temperature.

2. While in class, the teacher states that students will be working with a substance that is potentially combustible. Which of the following is not needed to work with this substance?

a. Safety goggles
b. Knowing the location of the fire extinguisher
c. Lab coat
d. Rubber boots

3. A student notices that every Monday the class has a quiz and that many of the students are not prepared. They begin to record the teacher's pattern of giving quizzes and notice that the quizzes fall on a Monday and cover the taught two weeks prior. What have the students noticed?

a. An observation
b. A trial
c. A trend
d. A model

Questions 4–5 pertain to the following chart:

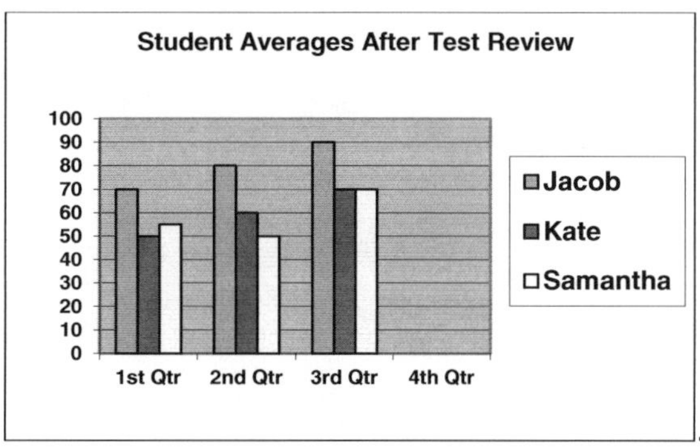

4. Using the table above, which student is likely to receive a 100% for the fourth quarter should this trend continue?

a. Jacob
b. Kate
c. Samantha
d. None of them

5. Using the table above, what conclusions can be made about the students' scores?

a. The scores increased as the year progressed
b. The girls did better than the boys on the test each quarter
c. The test was about Math
d. The scores were heavily impacted by the test reviews that were provided

6. In your garden, you noticed that the tomato plants did better on the North side of your house than the West side and you decided to figure out why. They are both planted with the same soil that provides adequate nutrients to the plant, and they are watered at the same time during the week. Over the course of a week, you begin to measure the amount of sunlight that hits each side of the house and determine that the North side gets more light because the sunlight is blocked by the house's shadow on the West side. What is the name of the factor in your observations that affected the tomato plants growth?

a. The control
b. The independent variable
c. The dependent variable
d. The conclusion

7. There are three insects that are being compared under a microscope. As a scientist, you decide that measuring them would be an important part of recording their data. Which unit of measurement would best for this situation?

a. Centimeters
b. Meters
c. Micrometers
d. Kilometers

8. A leading drug company has created a drug that can help cure diabetes, but before it can go on the market, the company must first prove that it works. The scientists use the drug on a group of 100 people and provide a placebo to another 100 people; neither group knows if they have received the drug or the placebo. All other factors, such as exercise, diet, and amount of sleep, have stayed the same. What is this experiment using to determine if the drug works?

a. A standard deviation
b. A dependent variable
c. A hypothesis
d. A control group

9. Which of the following is not provided as a result of the valid research and observations recorded by scientists?

a. A better understanding of the physical world
b. The ability to predict possible outcomes affected by actions
c. The ability to prevent earthquakes and other natural disasters
d. The creation of various substances and technologies that enhance our world

Question 10 pertains to the following table:

State Coyote Population, 1900-2010

Year	Population	Year	Population
1900	5,000	1960	50,000
1910	11,000	1970	70,000
1920	30,000	1980	50,000
1930	75,000	1990	40,000
1940	100,000	2000	20,000
1950	65,000	2010	8,000

10. In reference to the above table, if the state allowed hunting in only the highest populated years, what conclusions below would not have affected the continued decrease in population numbers from 1970 to 2010?

a. Scarcity of food sources
b. Migration to another area
c. The prohibition of coyote hunting
d. Reduction of shelter

11. In 1912, Alfred Wegener proposed that:

a. The earth's magnetic poles have reversed several times throughout history
b. Tectonic plates move because of convection currents in the mantle
c. Mountains are formed by tectonic plates pushing against one another
d. The continents once formed a single land mass, but have since drifted apart

12. While doing a chemistry experiment during class one of your friends gets splashed in the eye with a solution that you were mixing. What is the first thing you should do to help your friend?

a. Tell the teacher
b. Take your friend to the eyewash
c. Tell them to blink and that everything will be fine
d. Tell them to rub their eyes and then tell the teacher

13. What are goggles, lab aprons, and gloves called?

a. People protective equines
b. Personal protect equipment
c. Personal protective equipment
d. People protective equipment

14. After a laboratory experiment that involved using various chemical solutions, you and your lab partner are asked to clean up your workspace and dispose of any leftover chemicals. Unsure about the appropriate disposal method, you refer to which manual to find the best method for each solution?

a. Maternal Data Shifting Sheet
b. Maternal Data Safety Sheet
c. Materials Don't Shift Sheet
d. Safety Data Sheet

Question 15 pertains to the following diagram:

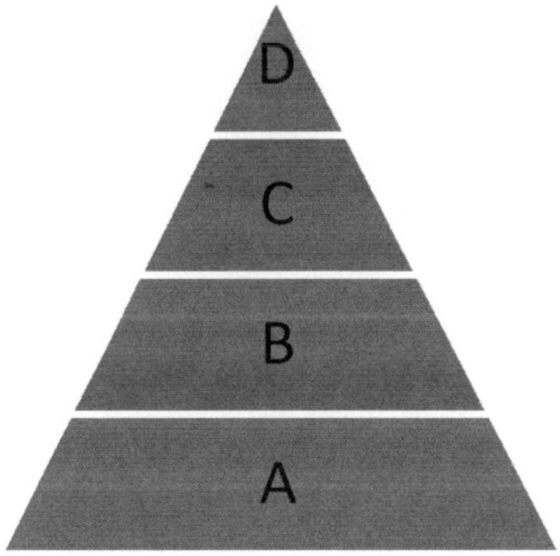

15. In the food chain pyramid above, which segment represents the placement of a coyote?

a. A (Producer)
b. B (Primary Consumer)
c. C (Secondary Consumer)
d. D (Decomposer)

16. All living things have:

a. Organelles
b. Cells
c. Tissues
d. Cell walls

17. The Gulf Oil Spill of 2010 deposited millions of gallons of crude oil into the wetlands of Louisiana, and many people in the area suffered. Which of the factors below was not among those drastically affected by the oil spill?

a. Water quality
b. Water temperature
c. Air quality
d. Presence of fish

18. What is the name of the process by which plants generate their own food source using sunlight, carbon dioxide, and water?

a. Photoemission
b. Chemotherapy
c. Chemosynthesis
d. Photosynthesis

19. In the marine waters, there is a beautiful, orange clown fish that lives closely with a sea anemone. This sea anemone can sting its prey with poisonous venom before devouring it; however, the clown fish is not affected by the sea anemone at all. The clown fish is only safe when hiding within the sea anemone's poisonous tentacles and protects the hiding spot from a certain type of fish who tries to eat the sea anemone. This is an example of what type of relationship?

a. Commensalism
b. Mutualism
c. Parasitism
d. None of the above

20. The sun provides a source of light for our planet, but it also plays an important role by heating the air and water, in turn causing atmospheric winds and ocean currents. The sun heats the air and water by ________.

a. Conduction
b. Radiation
c. Convection
d. None of the above

21. Which of the following is the most likely explanation for the reason finches on separate islands within an archipelago have differently shaped beaks?

a. Each bird evolved from a pre-existing ancestor on each island
b. The finches spread among the islands, but in small numbers, so genetic drift caused beak shape to change
c. Natural selection shaped the beaks in accordance with food availability on each island
d. The different finches were introduced by ancient humans

Question 22 pertains to the following diagram:

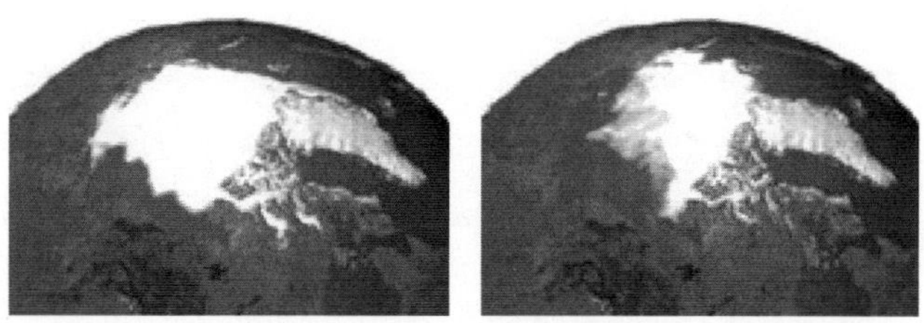

Arctic perennial sea ice has been decreasing at a rate of 9% per decade. The first image shows the minimum sea ice concentration for the year 1979, and the second image shows the minimum sea ice concentration in 2003.

22. The above images show the Arctic Circle in 1979 and in 2003. Which of the following would not be a short- or long-term effect of this change?

a. Impact on the ecological food pyramids and webs
b. Increase in sea levels
c. Diminished wetlands and marshes around the world
d. Increased global temperatures for the land and oceans

23. Which of the following situations would result in the generation of new crust?

a. Two crustal plates converge
b. Two crustal plates move apart
c. Two crustal plates slide past one another
d. A crustal plate is pushed down into the mantle

24. Which of the following is a property of nonmetals?

a. They are good conductors of electricity
b. They do not form isotopes
c. They react with metals
d. They are dense, hard, and have high melting points

25. The moon plays an important role in which of the following earth events?

a. Tides
b. Earthquakes
c. Earth's orbit
d. Northern Lights

26. The average distance from the earth to the sun is equal to one:

a. Astronomical unit
b. Light year
c. Parsec
d. Arcsecond

27. On your way to school you are carrying a book bag full of academic supplies, books, and lunch. What is causing the book bag to begin to feel very heavy as you walk to school?

a. The mass of the book bag
b. The weight of the book bag
c. The volume of the book bag
d. The size of the book bag

28. Cells are the smallest unit of a living organism; therefore, atoms would be the smallest unit of _____.

a. Matter
b. Mass
c. Weight
d. Periodic Table

29. Balance the following reaction between sulfuric acid and aluminum hydroxide by filling in the correct stoichiometric values for each chemical.

$$\_\ H_2SO_4 + \_\ Al(OH)_3 \rightarrow \_\ Al_2(SO_4)_3 + \_\ H_2O$$

a. 3, 2, 1, 6
b. 2, 3, 1, 3
c. 3, 3, 2, 6
d. 1, 2, 1, 4

30. What are the three main sections of the Periodic Table?

a. Metals, nonmetals, and gases
b. Metals, metalloids, and gases
c. Metals, nonmetals, and metalloids
d. Nonmetals, metalloids, and gases

31. Place your answer on the provided griddable answer sheet.

Using the Periodic Table, what is the total number of protons for iron?

32. Which answer balances the following equation?

$CO_2 + H_2O + \text{Energy} = C_6H_{12}O_6 + O_2$

a. $12CO_2 + 6H_2O + \text{Energy} = C_6H_{12}O_6 + 6O_2$
b. $6CO_2 + 6H_2O + \text{Energy} = 2C_6H_{12}O_6 + 12O_2$
c. $12CO_2 + 6H_2O + \text{Energy} = 2C_6H_{12}O_6 + 6O_2$
d. $6CO_2 + 6H_2O + \text{Energy} = C_6H_{12}O_6 + 6O_2$

33. Place your answer on the provided griddable answer sheet.

You are driving to your grandmother's house for her birthday. She lives 582 miles away. The average speed limit is 65mph. How long will it take you to get to your grandmother's house?

34. Most organic molecules have all of the following properties except

a. high solubility in water.
b. a relatively low melting point.
c. covalent bonds.
d. high flammability.

35. You are getting on a train bound for New York City, and your return trip will track at the same rate of speed. If you were going to determine your velocity, what would you need to know in addition to the speed of the trains?

a. Acceleration
b. Force
c. Direction
d. Reference point

36. A cheetah at rest is initially at 0m/s and then gets up to 2m/s once it begins to chase after an antelope. What is this change in velocity called?

a. Speed
b. Direction
c. Acceleration
d. Inertia

37. Which of the following is an example of a balanced force?

a. Two football players grabbing a football from the same direction
b. Two football players pushing on a football from opposite directions
c. A football player kicking the ball
d. A football player throwing the ball

38. Place your answer on the provided griddable answer sheet.

While driving in a car as a passenger, your mother stops abruptly in order to avoid hitting a hubcap in the road. After she slams on her brakes, you both move forward and then back once the seatbelt is activated. This is an example of which of Newton's Laws?

39. If the moon is at the point in its cycle where it is between the earth and the sun, which moon phase would we observe from the earth?

a. New moon
b. Last moon
c. Full moon
d. First quarter moon

40. When a cold front begins to overtake a warm front, this results in what type of front?

a. Stationary front
b. Occluded front
c. Cold front
d. Warm front

41. All of the following are examples of chemical changes in the digestive system except

a. Converting starches in carbohydrates to simple sugars
b. Protein digestion in the stomach
c. Chewing food into smaller pieces
d. Digestion of fat in the small intestine

42. The reason for seasonal changes on earth is because of the earth's revolution around the sun and which unique aspect of the earth?

a. The earth rotates around the moon
b. The earth is tilted at its equator
c. The earth is tilted at its axis
d. None of these

43. Many fishermen will watch the tide report for the local area and get up very early or stay out late in order to have the best fishing opportunity. Which factor affects the fisherman's fishing opportunities?

a. The gravitational relationship between the earth and moon
b. The gravitational relationship between the earth and sun
c. The earth's gravity
d. The moon's phases

44. In an amusement park ride, you stand on the floor of a cylindrical ring with your back touching the wall. The ring begins to rotate, slowly at first, but then faster and faster. When the ring is rotating fast enough, the floor is removed. You do not slide down but remained pressed against the wall of the ring. Which is the best explanation for why you don't fall down?

a. The centripetal force pushes you towards the wall
b. The centripetal force changes the direction of your motion
c. The force of friction between the wall and your body is greater than the force of gravity
d. The rotating ring creates a weightless environment

Question 45 pertains to the following diagram:

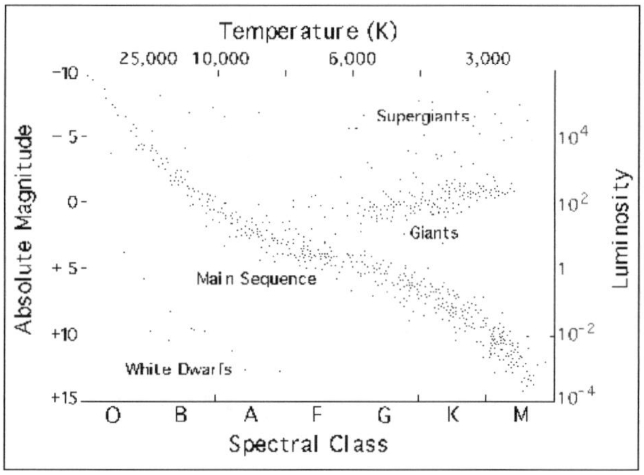

45. What is the name of the above figure used to classify stars based on temperature and luminosity?

a. Hershbrown-Russell diagram
b. Hertzsprung-Russell diagram
c. Hersheysrug-Russell diagram
d. None of the above

46. Place your answer on the provided griddable answer sheet.

100 g of ethanol C_2H_6O is dissolved in 100 g of water. The final solution has a volume of 0.2 L. What is the density of the resulting solution?

47. Identify the leaf shown below using the provided dichotomous key:

Step 1			
Is the leaf round?	Go to Step 2	Is the leaf long and skinny?	It is a Black Walnut

Step 2			
Does the leaf have smooth edges?	Go to Step 3	Does the leaf have saw tooth edges?	It is a Mulberry

Step 3			
Does the leaf have no lobes (fingers)?	It is a Dogwood	Does the leaf have lobes (fingers)?	It is a Sassafras

The leaf shown in the pictures is:

a. Black Walnut
b. Mulberry
c. Dogwood
d. Sassafras

48. Electromagnetic waves provide scientists with a way to determine the distance of an object by emitting pulses of radio waves and waiting for them to hit something in their path and bounce back. Which relation would you use to determine the distance of the object from the emitter?

a. Distance = mass/velocity
b. Force = mass * acceleration
c. Speed = distance/time
d. Work = Force * distance

49. When an animal takes in more energy than it uses over an extended time, the extra chemical energy is stored as:

a. Fat
b. Starch
c. Protein
d. Enzymes

50. What is primary driving force in the development a hurricane?

a. High winds
b. Ocean temperatures
c. Cloud cover
d. Contact with land

51. Prokaryotic and eukaryotic cells are similar in having which of the following?

a. Membrane-bound organelles
b. Protein-studded DNA
c. Presence of a nucleus
d. Integral membrane proteins in the plasma membrane

52. Which of the following organisms is capable of undergoing asexual reproduction?

a. Ferns
b. Yeast
c. Flowering plants
d. Trees

53. The brain is part of the:

a. Integumentary system
b. Nervous system
c. Endocrine system
d. Respiratory system

54. Genetics is the study of:

a. Anatomy
b. Physiology
c. Heredity
d. Science

Answer Key and Explanations

1. A: Temperature affects a molecule in two ways. Hotter temperatures cause molecules expand and move apart from each other; colder temperatures make them shrink and pull together, just like you would on a cold day. The answer is (A) because the mercury molecules will expand on a hotter day, causing the mercury to rise up the thermometer.

2. D: Students should know where to locate a fire extinguisher should a small fire should start. If it is too large to contain, they should immediately exit the building and call 911. Students should wear lab coats and safety goggles to protect clothing and eyes from any spillage of the substance and to reduce the chance of it getting into their eyes. Rubber boots would not be as protective as the lab coat and goggles.

3. C: A trend is the foreseeable pattern of an observed event. In this case, the students began to observe the teacher giving a quiz every Monday covering the material presented two weeks prior; therefore, they observed a trend.

4. A: According to the table, Jacob started with a 70% and has consistently moved up 10% with each quarter, as has Kate, but she started at 60%. Samantha started at 55% and has not always increased her scores. Should this trend continue, Jacob will most likely earn a 100%.

5. A: The table reflects student scores for each quarter. The trend that can be seen in the graph is an increase in scores as the year progressed. The graph label mentions a test review, but there is not enough information about that to know if that is the reason for the scores changing.

6. B: The conclusion was that the amount of sunlight received by the plants was affecting their growth. The independent variable was the amount of light that was given to the plants and could have been manipulated by the experimenter by moving the plants or adding equal parts of light. No control was used in this experiment.

7. C: The best use of the International System of Units (SI) for this situation would be the use of the micrometer as it is the smallest unit of measurement provided and the scientist is using a microscope to view the insects.

8. D: The drug company has provided all of the same variables to the two groups with the exception of one group receiving the drug and the other taking the placebo. The group on the drug is experimental; the placebo is a control group.

9. C: Scientists make observations, gather data, and complete research over many years in order to compile knowledge that will provide insight into future disasters, such as earthquakes, storms, and global warming. Although science can be used to predict earthquakes and other natural disasters, there is currently no way of preventing them from occurring.

10. C: Although no data is shown that reflects the years in which hunting licenses were sold, the prohibition of hunting would allow a population to increase its numbers. The coyote's populations would suffer without adequate food sources or shelter, and migration would reduce it as well.

11. D: In 1912, Alfred Wegener proposed that the continents once formed a single land mass called Pangaea, but have since drifted apart. Theories about the earth's magnetic fields and plate tectonics did not emerge until years later. Once they did, they helped produce evidence to support Wegener's theory.

12. B: The first thing you should do is assist your friend to the eyewash. After, or if possible while, doing this, you should get the attention of the teacher. Depending on the solution that was introduced into the eye, every second counts to maintain the integrity of the eye itself and its vision. Rubbing or blinking may further irritate the eye and cause more damage.

13. C: Goggles, lab aprons, and gloves are personal protective equipment for an individual to wear as protection against splashing solutions onto clothing or skin or into the eyes and should be worn while working with any chemicals or flammable materials.

14. D: While some chemicals can be poured down the drain safely without affecting the pipes or the environment, not all can. Therefore, by reading about the chemical in the Safety Data Sheet (SDS), you can determine if it is caustic, flammable, or harmful to the environment if poured down the drain.

15. C: The diagram represents an ecological pyramid. The letter A represents the producers, such as plants. The letter B represents the primary consumers usually herbivores. The letter C stands for the secondary consumers, the carnivores that feed on the herbivores. A coyote is a carnivore and would, therefore, be in this group and represented by the letter C. The pyramid's fourth level, represented by a D, includes the decomposers, such as bacteria and fungi, which decompose dead organic material.

16. B: Cells are the basic units of life, and all organisms have them. Some organisms like bacteria have just a single cell, while complex organisms like humans have hundreds of trillions. Prokaryotes do not have organelles Not all organisms have tissues, groups of cells that make up connective tissue, muscle tissue, etc. Finally, only some types of cells, including plant cells, have cell walls d.

17. B: All of the factors above were drastically affected by the oil spill except the temperature of the water. Oil did not significantly impact the temperature of the water. The spill did impact the water quality and air quality by the introduction of oil and other chemicals from the cleanup into the water and air. The presence of the oil also killed or drove away many of the fish that would otherwise have been near the gulf coast.

18. D: Photosynthesis is the process by which plants generate their own food (glucose), using sunlight, water, and carbon dioxide. Oxygen is also generated as a byproduct.

19. B: The relationship between the clown fish and the sea anemone is an example of mutualism - because both organisms are benefitting from the relationship. The Clown fish gains the protection from the anemone while offering protection to the anemone from being eaten by a certain type of fish.

20. B: Radiation is the heat energy that is transferred from electromagnetic waves such as the sun. Convection is the transfer of heat energy within a gas or liquid substance because of circulation. Conduction is the transfer of heat by direct contact. Once the air and water have been heated, they move and circulate because of the difference in the density of hot and cold water and of hot and cold air.

21. C: Finches with beaks well-suited for the types of food available on an island had an evolutionary advantage. As a result, these finches survived and reproduced, a phenomenon known as natural selection. The finches share a common ancestor, regardless of the island on which they now live. Genetic drift refers to genetic changes that occur due to random chance; this would not account for different beaks on different islands. Introduction by humans would not account for different beaks, since phenotypes change over time.

22. C: The melting of the Arctic Circle would mean that sea levels would increase and wetlands and marshes would then become flooded with seawater. This would lead to the death of many plant and animal species within those ecosystems. Global temperatures would not decrease but would increase on both the land and oceans.

23. B: When two crustal plates move apart, magma welling up could result in the formation of new crust. This has been shown to be occurring on the ocean floor where places of the crust are weaker. The crust spreads apart at these trenches, pushing outward and erupting at the ridges. When two crustal plates converge, sublimation occurs as one plate runs under another pushing it up. Two crustal plates slide past one another, is an example of a transform fault, which does not create new crust. A crustal plate is pushed down into the mantle, does not form new crust but perhaps recycles the old one.

24. C: Nonmetal ions are negatively charged, while metal ions are positively charged. Because of these opposite charges, they readily bond and react. The metal iron, for instance, reacts readily with the nonmetal oxygen to form rust. As a general rule, nonmetals are considered nonconductors Nonmetals, including oxygen, can form isotopes. Nonmetals typically have low densities, are not hard, and have low melting points.

25. A: The moon's gravitational pull against the earth causes the earth's oceans to bulge out at the points nearest to and farthest from the moon, causing the displacement of water that occurs twice a day, known as high and low tide.

26. A: The average distance from the earth to the sun is equal to one astronomical unit (AU). An AU is equal to 93 million miles, and is far smaller than a light year or a parsec. A light year is defined as the distance light can travel in a vacuum in one year, and is equal to roughly 64,341 AU. A parsec is the parallax of one arcsecond, and is equal to $206.26 \times 10^{\Delta 3}$ astronomical units.

27. B: Weight and mass are very similar but differ in that mass is the amount of matter something contains and can be measured in grams and weight is affected by the gravitational pull of the object. Weight is the answer because gravity is pulling on the book bag, making it feel heavier than it really is.

28. A: Atoms are the smallest and most basic unit of matter. When combined, they form elements just as cells of the same type form tissues.

29. A: By comparing the products to the reactants, there must be at least two Al atoms in the starting material, and at least three sulfate groups. Therefore, a coefficient of 2 must be placed in front of $Al(OH)_3$ and a coefficient of 3 must be placed in front of H_2SO_4. To make the number of hydrogen and oxygen atoms equal on both sides of the equation, a coefficient of 6 must be placed in front of H_2O.

30. C: The Periodic Table systematically arranges elements according to their properties, and many of the properties are more reactive than others. The most reactive are the metals, which are found on the left side of the table. The least reactive are the nonmetals, found on the right. In between the metals and nonmetals are the metalloids, which share some of the properties of both groups.

31. 26: On the Periodic Table, iron (Fe) has an atomic number of 26 and an atomic mass of 55.847. The atomic number indicates the number of protons that the element has within its nucleus. The atomic mass is the average mass of the isotopes within that element. The answer is 26 protons because the atomic number is 26.

32. D: The equation $6CO_2 + 6H_2O$ + Energy = $C_6H_{12}O_6 + 6O_2$ (photosynthesis) can be balanced by counting the number of each element on the reactant side and comparing those totals to the product side. There should be equal numbers of each element on both sides, and they can be adjusted by changing the coefficient to add another molecule to the formula to balance the other side. The formula above represents photosynthesis and has six more CO_2 molecules on its reactant side than usual; thus, additional glucose and oxygen molecules will be produced.

33. 9 hours: The formula for calculating speed is S=D/T. However, you are looking for time, so you would divide distance (D) by speed (S) to get the time (T). The answer is 9 hours.

34. A: Most organic molecules are not highly soluble in water. A low melting point, covalent bonds, and high flammability are all characteristics of organic molecules. Organic molecules are those that contain carbon molecules, with a few exceptions. Organic molecules tend to be less soluble in water than inorganic salts. They are good at forming unique structures and there are many organic compounds. Examples of organic compounds include hydrocarbons, carbohydrates, lipids, and proteins.

35. C: Velocity is the speed of an object going in a specific direction; therefore, the answer is direction.

36. C: Acceleration is the change in an object's velocity. Velocity is the direction and speed in which an object is moving.

37. B: A balanced force is one that has no net force being applied to an object; therefore, it does not move. The two football players that are pushing on the football from opposite directions are applying force from both sides so that the ball does not move, making it a balanced force.

38. First: Newton's First Law is the law of inertia, which states an object will continue in the direction that it was traveling until acted upon. In this case, your body continued to move forward until your seatbelt stopped you, acting as an unbalanced force.

39. A: A new moon is one that is in between the earth and sun. The moon would then receive light on the side closest to the sun and its illuminated sides would not be directly visible to us on the earth.

40. B: An occluded front occurs when a cold front has overtaken a warm front, resulting in a mature storm system. A stationary front does not move. A cold front brings cold air, while a warm front brings warm air.

41. C: Chewing food into smaller pieces is a physical change, not a chemical change.

42. C: The earth experiences seasons because it revolves around the sun while tilted on its axis, exposing one hemisphere to the sun more than the other hemisphere. The hemisphere closest to the sun will be experiencing summer, while the other hemisphere has winter. The Northern Hemisphere and Southern Hemisphere experience opposite seasons all year long.

43. A: The rising and falling of the ocean's tides are directly influenced by the gravitational pull of the moon on the earth. High tide is found in areas closest and farthest from the moon because the moon pulls the water and earth toward it, leaving the water on the other side of the earth behind. Low tide occurs in the areas not affected by high tide. There are two tides each day.

44. C: The centripetal force pushes you in toward the center of the ring, not towards the wall. The centripetal force also causes the ring to push against you, which is why it might feel like you're being pushed outwards. This force also causes friction between your back and the wall, and that is why you don't fall when the floor is removed, assuming the frictional force is large enough to overcome gravity. As the speed of rotation increases, the force exerted by the wall on your body increases, so the frictional force between you and the wall increases. Centripetal force does cause you to change direction—but it does not explain why you don't fall. Also note that "centrifugal force" is an illusion; because you feel the wall pushing against your back, you feel like you're being pushed outwards. In fact, you're being pulled inwards, but the wall is also being pulled inwards and is pushing against you. Finally, you are not weightless on a ride like this.

45. B: The Hertzsprung-Russell diagram was named after the designers Ejnar Hertzsprung and Henry Norris Russell. The diagram plots stars based on their spectral class or temperature and magnitude or luminosity.

46. 1 g/mL: Density is determined by dividing the mass of the solution by its volume. The mass is 200 g, and the total volume is 0.2 L, or 200 mL. So 200 g/200 mL = 1 g/mL.

47. B: A mulberry leaf is round in shape and has saw tooth edges. Following the dichotomous key helps to identify the leaf based on its physical characteristics.

48. C: The formula for calculating speed is distance over time. Since we know the speed of the waves and the time it took to get to the object and back, we can calculate the distance.

49. A: Long-term energy storage in animals takes the form of fat. Animals also store energy as glycogen, and plants store energy as starch, but these substances are for shorter-term use. Fats are a good storage form for chemical energy because fatty acids bond to glycerol in a condensation reaction to form fats (triglycerides). This reaction, which releases water, allows for the compacting of high-energy fatty acids in a concentrated form.

50. B: Hurricanes are primarily formed because of the temperature difference between the oceans and the atmospheric air. The oceans heat up during the summer months and once they climb above 80 degrees Fahrenheit, the conditions are ideal for a hurricane. Evaporation of the warm water forms clouds, which then expand into storm clouds. Atmospheric winds help push the storm over warmer waters, allowing it to grow. A hurricane will die if introduced to cold waters or cut off from a water source.

51. D: Both prokaryotes and eukaryotes interact with the extracellular environment and use membrane-bound or membrane-associated proteins to achieve this. They both use diffusion and active transport to move materials in and out of their cells. Prokaryotes have very few proteins associated with their DNA, whereas eukaryotes' DNA is richly studded with proteins. Both types of living things can have flagella, although with different structural characteristics in the two groups. The most important differences between prokaryotes and eukaryotes are the lack of a nucleus and membrane-bound organelles in prokaryotes.

52. B: Asexual reproduction means that offspring are produced by a single parent. Yeast cells reproduce asexually through budding. The genetic material of the cell is copied, and a small bud forms on the outside of the yeast cell. It grows and eventually breaks away, forming a new yeast cell. Most organisms, including ferns, flowering plants, and trees, require two parents to produce seeds, spores, etc. In other words, they are not capable of asexual reproduction.

53. B: The brain is part of the nervous system.

54. C: Genetics is the study of heredity.

Practice Test #2

1. Which of the following elements are ordered from least reactive to most reactive according to the Periodic Table?

a. Ar, Cu, Na
b. Na, Ar, Cu
c. Na, Cu, Ar
d. Ar, Na, Cu

2. The group of elements that contains most of the semiconductors is called?

a. Metals
b. Metalloids
c. Nonmetals
d. Noble gases

3. Place your answer on the provided griddable answer sheet.

In the chemical formula for glucose, $5C_6H_{12}O_6$, which number represents a coefficient?

4. Which of the following answers shows $CH_4 + O_2 = CO_2 + H_2O$ as balanced?

a. $CH_4 + 2O_2 = 2CO_2 + 2H_2O$
b. $2CH_4 + 4O_2 = 2CO_2 + H_2O$
c. $2CH_4 + O_2 = 2CO_2 + H_2O$
d. $CH_4 + 2O_2 = CO_2 + 2H_2O$

5. Identify the leaf shown below using the provided dichotomous key:

Step 1			
Is the leaf irregular, but symmetrical?	Go to Step 2	Is the leaf long and skinny?	It is a Black Walnut

Step 2			
Does the leaf have smooth edges?	Go to Step 3	Does the leaf have saw tooth edges?	It is a Mulberry

Step 3			
Does the leaf have no lobes (fingers)?	It is a Dogwood	Does the leaf have lobes (fingers)?	It is a Sassafras

The leaf shown in the pictures is:

a. Black Walnut
b. Mulberry
c. Dogwood
d. Sassafras

6. Evidence of a chemical reaction can be determined by all of the following except?

a. Modifying the arrangement of atoms
b. Endothermic and exothermic reactions
c. Equal masses of reactants and products
d. No change in energy

7. Two boys on skateboards decide to race to the end of the street. Both travel the same distance but arrive at different times. This example illustrates which concept?

a. Direction
b. Acceleration
c. Speed
d. Velocity

8. Place your answer on the provided griddable answer sheet.

Aubrey lives 200m from Brianna's house. If it takes her 100s to travel the distance, what is Aubrey's speed?

9. Which of the following devices changes chemical energy into electrical energy?

a. Battery
b. Closed electric circuit
c. Generator
d. Transformer

10. In the store, you are pushing a cart with no problem. However, as you are shopping, you add items to the cart that have varying masses. Which of Newton's Laws play a role in the amount of force needed to push the cart through the store?

a. Newton's First Law
b. Newton's Second Law
c. Newton's Third Law
d. Newton's Fourth Law

11. You are watching the Olympic ice skating championships and see the pairs are up next. They begin their routine facing each other with their palms up and against each other. When the music starts they push themselves apart with their palms. What type of force is this?

a. Magnetic
b. Balanced
c. Action and reaction force
d. Centripetal force

12. Two rabbits are getting ready to jump across the field away from a predator. One of the rabbits is about twice the size of the other. As they bound away, which of the rabbits will have to exert more force on its jumps and why?

a. The smaller rabbit, because its legs are shorter
b. The smaller rabbit, because it will have to take more jumps to escape the predator
c. The larger rabbit, because it has more mass that must overcome gravity and accelerate
d. The larger rabbit, because it has more air resistance to deal with

13. Light waves are an example of which type of wave?

a. Longitudinal
b. Transverse
c. Compressional
d. None of the above

14. Place your answer on the provided griddable answer sheet.

Substance A has a density of 5.0 kg/m^3 and substance B has a density of 4.0 kg/m^3. What is the ratio of volume A to volume B when the masses of the two substances are equal?

15. Which of the following is an example of visible light that travels through space and produces heat?

a. Bioluminescence light
b. Incandescent light
c. Sunlight
d. Fluorescent light

16. Which of the following is not an example of a renewable resource?

a. Sunlight
b. Crude oil
c. Wind
d. Tide

17. Coral reefs are an important ecosystem within the world's oceans. They act as a filtering system, reduce the amount of carbon dioxide in the water, provide shelter for many organisms, and offer economic benefits to many people around the world. However, coral reefs are in danger of being irreversibly destroyed. Which of the following is not a cause of the destruction of coral reefs?

a. Reattachment of salvaged coral colonies on the reef
b. Global warming
c. Collection of coral by people to sell
d. Water pollution

18. The sun sits on the edge of which galaxy?

a. Milky Way
b. Elliptical Galaxy
c. Irregular Galaxy
d. Doppler Galaxy

Question 20 pertains to the following table:

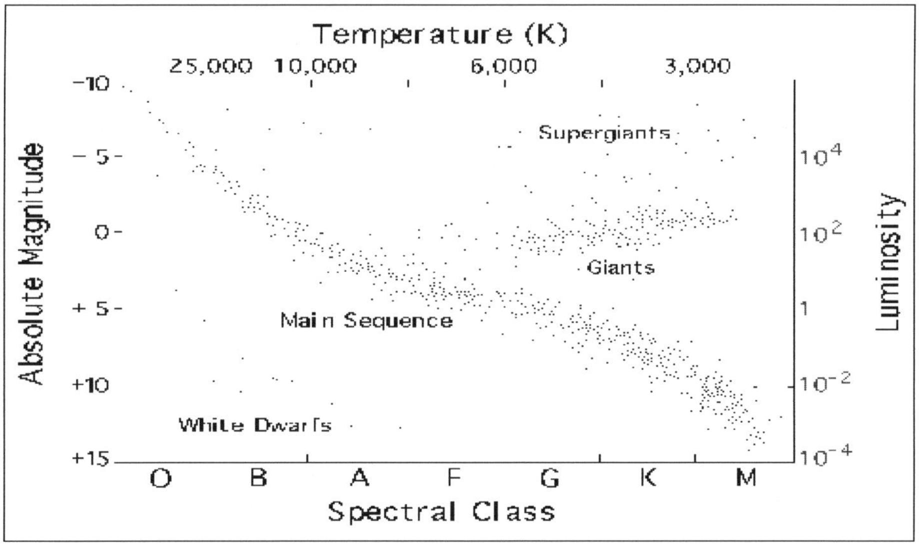

19. According to the diagram above, what unit of measurement is used to determine the star temperature?

a. Celsius
b. Kelvin
c. Fahrenheit
d. None of the above

20. Which of the following is a star with an absolute magnitude of +10 and a temperature of 25,000K?

a. Main Sequence
b. Super Giant
c. Giant
d. White Dwarf

21. Which statement correctly states the work-energy theorem?

a. The change in kinetic energy of an object is equal to the work done by the object
b. The change in kinetic energy of an object is equal to the work done on an object
c. The change in potential energy of an object is equal to the work done by the object
d. The change in potential energy of an object is equal to the work done on an object

22. Which of the following below is not considered evidence of plate tectonics?

a. The shape of continents fits together like a puzzle
b. Fossil comparisons exist along where the continents would fit together
c. The Mid-Atlantic Ridge shows where new crust is formed
d. There is a large amount of inland seismic activity

23. Earth's oceans have many little waves that are caused by the various wind speeds around the globe. However, one type of wave is caused by a celestial body. Which celestial body causes this wave?

a. Sun
b. Stars
c. Planets
d. Moon

24. On December 22 of every year, the people in the southern hemisphere of the earth experience which event?

a. Summer Solstice
b. Winter Solstice
c. Spring Equinox
d. Fall Equinox

25. The atomic number of an element is determined by:

a. The number of neutrons in the nucleus of an atom
b. The number of protons in the nucleus of an atom
c. The number of protons plus the number of neutrons in an atom
d. The number of protons plus the number of electrons in an atom

26. A tapeworm lives within another organism and feeds off the nutrients that are ingested by that organism. At times, this can cause the organism to experience malnutrition or death. This is an example of what type of relationship?

a. Predator/prey
b. Symbiosis
c. Parasite/host
d. Producer/consumer

27. In a pond, eutrophication, the pollution of water by plant nutrients, can occur, causing chemical, biological, and ecological changes to the pond. As plant material begins to decompose and carbon dioxide begins to increase, what would happen to the fish in the pond?

a. They would flourish
b. They would relocate to another area
c. They would die off
d. They would not be affected

28. In Lake Erie, a species of fish called the Blue Pike was overfished one year. The following year, there was a pollution incident that killed off another large portion of the population. These events, combined with the previous year's overfishing of adult fish, led to the extinction of the Blue Pike species—none of the other species were affected. What happened to other fish species in the lake over time after the Blue Pike became extinct?

a. They became extinct
b. They were not affected by the other species' fate
c. Their numbers increased due to lack of competition
d. Their numbers decreased due to lack of competition

29. Our planet's oceans are experiencing climate changes, pollution, and overfishing. Which of the following answers is not a result of human activity?

a. Diminishment of coral reefs
b. Destruction of food webs
c. Increased population of all species
d. Degradation or total loss of wetlands

30. Which section of the digestive system is responsible for water reabsorption?

a. The large intestine
b. The duodenum
c. The small intestine
d. The gallbladder

31. All of the following are examples of physical changes in the digestive system except:

a. Squeezing the food through the esophagus
b. Drinking to help aid in swallowing food
c. Chewing food into smaller pieces
d. Digestion of fat in the small intestine

32. Which moon phase is the opposite moon phase of a new moon?

a. New moon
b. Last moon
c. Full moon
d. First quarter moon

33. Two species of finches are able to utilize the same food supply, but their beaks are different. They are able to coexist on an island because of:

a. Niche overlap
b. Character displacement
c. Resource partitioning
d. Realized niches

34. In mosses, eggs and sperm are produced by:

a. Spores
b. Sporophytes
c. Gametophytes
d. Zygotes

35. You and a lab partner will be completing a scientific experiment measuring the mass of chewed gum after one-minute chewing increments. Which lab equipment will you most likely use?

a. Triple beam balance
b. Anemometer
c. Hot plate
d. Microscope

36. A triple beam balance would show the units of measurement in which form?

a. Liters
b. Grams
c. Meters
d. Gallons

37. All of the following are examples of controlling eukaryotic gene expression EXCEPT

a. Regulatory proteins
b. Nucleosome packing
c. Methylation of DNA
d. Operons

38. Mrs. Jones's class conducted an experiment on the effects of sugar and artificial sweetener on the cookie recipe's overall color when baked. What would be the independent variable in the cookie experiment?

a. The students should use the same ingredients in both recipes, but bake the cookies with sugar at 450 degrees and those with artificial sweetener at 475 degrees. They should increase the baking time on the artificial sweetener cookies, since the package instructs them to do so
b. The students should use the same ingredients in both recipes, but increase the baking time on the artificial sweetener cookies, since the package instructs them to do so
c. The students should only vary the sugar or sweetener and otherwise use the same ingredients, same baking temperatures, and same baking times for both recipes
d. The students should use the same ingredients and baking times in both recipes, but bake the cookies with sugar at 450 degrees and the artificial sweetener cookies at 475 degrees

39. In the suburban neighborhood of Northwoods, there have been large populations of deer, and residents have complained about them eating flowers and garden plants. What would be a logical explanation, based on observations, for the large increase in the deer population over the last two seasons?

a. Increased quantity of food sources
b. Decreased population of a natural predator
c. Deer migration from surrounding areas
d. Increase in hunting licenses sold

Questions 40-42 pertain to the following passage:

> Your class is competing with another class to determine who can produce the tallest plants. Your class decides to test a couple of solutions to determine which would be best for overall plant growth before competing. Starting with four sets of four plants, the class decides to water each set with a different solution. They water them once a week with 200ml of the following solutions: water, diet soda, 1% bleach solution, and a 1% salt solution. All plants are placed in the window that receives the recommended amount of light. After a month of testing, your class notices that only two plants are alive, but one of those two does not look healthy.

40. What is the independent variable used in the plant growth experiment?

a. 200 ml quantity of solution
b. Amount of sunlight provided
c. Number of times the plants are watered
d. The type of solution applied to the plants

41. Based on these results, which of the following would be a good hypothesis to design the next experiment around?

a. Plants need more than 200 mL of liquid per week.
b. Salt has no impact on plant health.
c. Salt contains useful nutrients for plants.
d. A combination of the solutions tested will produce healthier plants.

42. What is the control, if any, in this experiment?

a. There is no control in this experiment
b. The control is the water
c. The control is the diet soda
d. The control is the amount of sunlight provided to the plants

43. What is a hypothetical explanation for an occurrence that is based on prior knowledge called?

a. Independent variable
b. Dependent variable
c. Trial
d. Hypothesis

44. What lab equipment would most likely be used to measure a liquid solution?

a. Flask
b. Triple beam balance
c. Graduated cylinder
d. Test tube

45. Which answer below represents the first steps in the scientific investigation process?

a. Construct a hypothesis and test with experiment
b. Analyze results and draw conclusions
c. Report results
d. Ask a question about a problem and do background research

46. During a chemistry experiment, which of the data below would not be collected for your lab report?

a. Temperature changes
b. Color changes
c. Production of gas or odor
d. Observations of other trials

47. What preventative safety equipment is required when working with flammable materials?

a. Apron
b. Fire blanket and extinguisher
c. Eye wash station
d. Goggles

48. What kind of graph would be best to represent data from an experiment with repeated trials comparing the speed of a car and the distance it traveled over time?

a. Pie graph
b. Bar graph
c. Line graph
d. Scatter plot graph

Question 49 pertains to the following chart:

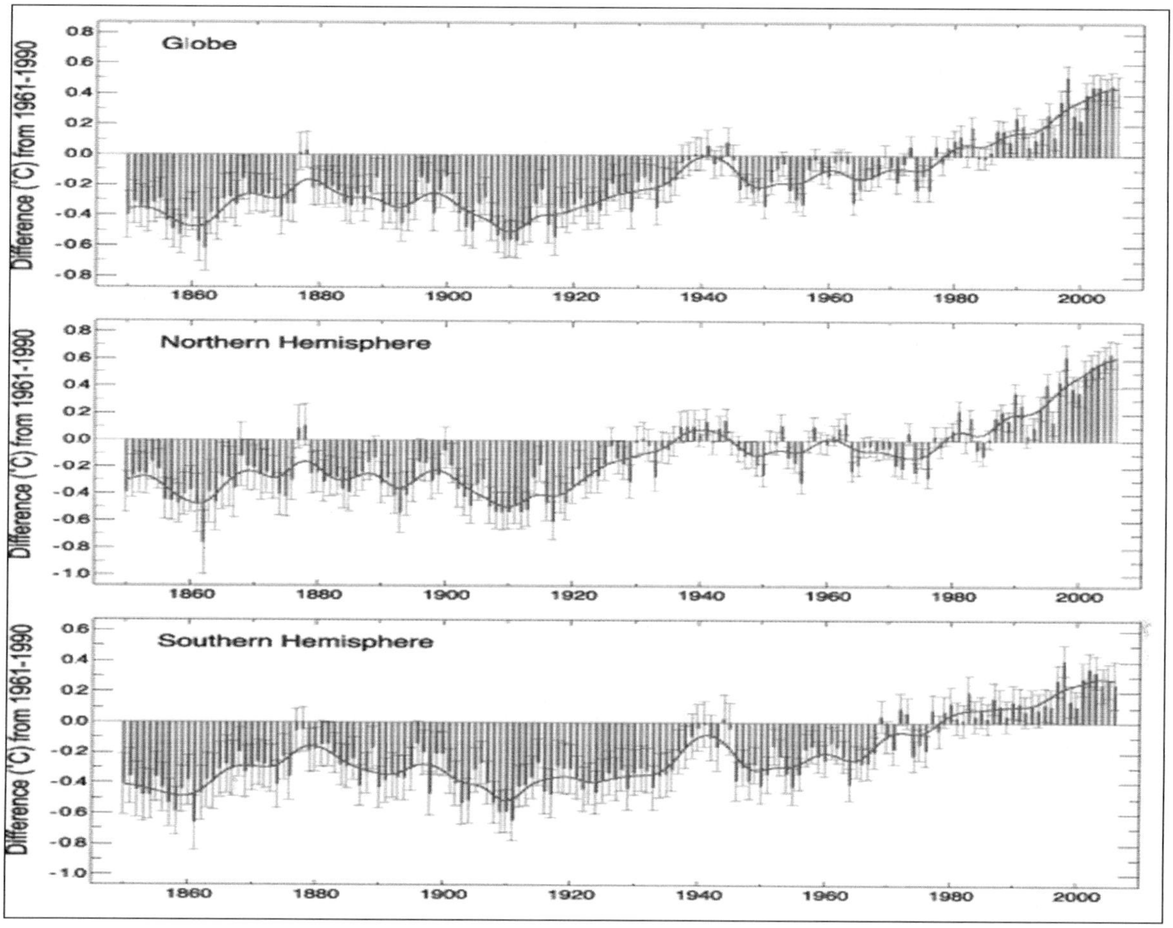

49. The above data table shows the increase of global warming from 1860 to 2000. Which portion of the globe has had the most effect on global warming?

a. Southern Hemisphere
b. Northern Hemisphere
c. Western Hemisphere
d. Eastern Hemisphere

50. The part of the human excretory system most responsible for maintaining normal body temperature is the:

a. Kidney
b. Bladder
c. Liver
d. Sweat glands

51. Of the following, which is the most basic unit of matter?

a. A helium atom
b. A sodium ion
c. A proton
d. An oxygen molecule

52. Which of the following is NOT true for all cells?

a. Cells are the basic structures of any organism
b. Cells can only reproduce from existing cells
c. Cells are the smallest unit of any life form that carries the information needed for all life processes
d. All cells are also called eukaryotes

53. In which of the following scenarios is Mario not applying work to a book?

a. Mario moves a book from the floor to the top shelf of a bookcase
b. Mario lets go of a book that he is holding so that it falls to the floor
c. Mario pushes a box of books across the room
d. Mario balances a book on his head and walks across the room

54. Place your answer on the provided griddable answer sheet.

You blow up a rubber balloon and hold the opening tight with your fingers. You then release your fingers, causing air to blow out of the balloon. This pushes the balloon forward, causing the balloon shoots across the room. Which of Newton's laws best explains the cause of this motion?

Answer Key and Explanations

1. A: The Periodic Table's two most reactive groups are Group 1 and Group 17; therefore, Na, found in Group 1, would be the most reactive of the three elements. The element Cu is found in Group 11, which marks it as a transition metal, and is only somewhat reactive. Group 18, which includes Ar, contains the Noble Gases, which are not at all reactive.

2. B: An element that has semi-conductive properties would be a metalloid. Metals are good conductors of electricity and heat. In contrast, nonmetals and the noble gases are not good conductors of electricity and heat. A semi-conductor is one that will conduct electricity under some conditions, but not others.

3. 5: In the formula for glucose, the numbers 6 and 12 both represent subscripts. A subscript represents the number of molecules for that specific element present in the formula. The C, H, and O are symbols for the elements Carbon, Hydrogen, and Oxygen, respectively. A coefficient is the number in front of the formula and represents the total number of molecules; in this formula there are five glucose molecules.

4. D: For the formula $CH_4 + O_2 = CO_2 + H_2O$ to be balanced there must be an equal number of molecules on both the reactant and product sides. In this case, for the formula to be balanced, a coefficient of a 2 needs to be placed in front of the O_2 and the H_2O molecules.

5. D: A sassafras leaf is irregular in shape but symmetrical. It also has smooth edges and finger like lobes. Following the dichotomous key helps to identify the leaf based on its physical characteristics.

6. D: A chemical reaction will always have an endothermic (absorb energy) or exothermic (release energy) reaction, and a chemical formula must always be balanced. Therefore, the masses of the reactants and products will always be equal, resulting in the modification of the atoms arrangement and a change in energy.

7. C: Speed is the distance at which something travels within a given time. The example states that both skateboarders traveled the same distance but arrived at different time. Therefore, they traveled at different speeds.

8. 2 m/s: The formula to calculate speed is S=D/T. In this problem, divide 200m by 100s, which gives you 2m/s.

9. A: In a Zn-Cu battery, the zinc terminal has a higher concentration of electrons than the copper terminal, so there is a potential difference between the locations of the two terminals. This is a form of electrical energy brought about by the chemical interactions between the metals and the electrolyte the battery uses. Creating a circuit and causing a current to flow will transform the electrical energy into heat energy, mechanical energy, or another form of electrical energy, depending on the devices in the circuit. A generator transforms mechanical energy into electrical energy, and a transformer changes the electrical properties of a form of electrical energy.

10. B: Newton's Second Law states that the acceleration of an object is increased by the force applied and decreased by its mass. As the cart becomes heavier through the store, the shopper must apply more force when pushing it to achieve its acceleration. Newton's First Law states if an object is at rest, it will stay at rest until a force is acted upon it. Newton's Third Law states that any object that exerts a force will be met by an equal opposing force. There is no Fourth Law.

11. C: The ice skaters are applying Newton's Third Law to create an equal and opposite reaction force, causing both partners to move. Although each skater is pushing the other, there is another force that must be considered in that they moved as well.

12. C: The larger rabbit, because it has more mass that must overcome gravity and accelerate. Newton's Second Law states that the force required to accelerate a body is directly proportional to its mass. Thus, the larger rabbit will have to exert more force on the ground to achieve the same level of acceleration as the smaller rabbit.

13. B: A transverse wave is one in which the oscillation is perpendicular to the direction of motion. Light waves are made up of an electric field and magnetic field which both oscillate perpendicular to the direction of motion and to one another.

14. 4/5 or 0.8: The density of an object is its mass divided by its volume. One easy way to work this problem is to select a convenient mass for both substances and compare the volumes. If you have 20 kg of both materials, you will have 4.0 m^3 of A and 5.0 m^3 of B. The ratio of the volume of A to the volume of B is 4/5 or 0.8.

15. C: Sunlight is a source of visible light and produces heat that is transferred throughout space. Bioluminescence is a visible light created by living things, but it does not produce heat like incandescent lights do. Fluorescent lights are an artificial light source created by man and require electricity to function.

16. B: Renewable resources are those resources whose supplies can replenish naturally as quickly as or more quickly than they are consumed. Examples of renewable resources are sunlight, tides, and wind, which occur naturally and are plentiful. Fossil fuels take many years to form and are currently being consumed faster than they are being produced.

17. A: Coral reefs are destroyed by increased temperatures resulting from global warming and water pollution, which suffocates the coral as algae grows over it. Illegal collection and sale of coral to restaurants, pet stores, and others have depleted healthy colonies. Many conservation efforts include enacting international laws protecting the reefs, creating natural parks, and reattaching salvaged coral colonies on the reef with the hopes of reconstructing the reef have been started in recent years.

18. A: The sun is located in our galaxy, the Milky Way, which is a spiral-shaped galaxy. Elliptical and Irregular Galaxies are examples of other galaxy shapes. There is no Doppler Galaxy.

19. B: The Hertzsprung-Russell diagram uses the Kelvin International System of Units (SI) measurement to measure the temperature of a star,

20. D: White Dwarf stars are found at the lower left-hand corner of the Hertzsprung-Russell diagram and can be plotted by following the 10+ magnitude and a temperature of 25,000K until the two points meet.

21. B: The work-energy theorem can be written $W = \Delta KE$. It is derived from Newton's second law ($F = ma$) by multiplying both sides by the distance the object moves. This work is the work done by a force on an object, and not the work done by an object. Work is only done by an object if that object exerts a force on another object, causing a change in its kinetic energy or position. The work done on an object may equal its potential energy, but only if that potential energy is converted into kinetic energy. In real-life cases, some energy is converted to heat, for example, so the change in potential energy does not equal the change in kinetic energy.

22. D: Evidence of plate tectonics is based on the shapes of the continents, which seem to fit together like a puzzle, as well as the fossils found along these edges. The Mid-Atlantic Ridge is the birthplace of new crust that is then destroyed in the subduction zones in the Pacific Ring of Fire, where most seismic activity takes place.

23. D: Although all of the answers are celestial bodies, natural bodies outside of the earth's atmosphere, only one influences the earth's tides. The moon's gravitational pull on the earth causes the seas to rise and fall as one large wave, known as a tide, with a very large wavelength as compared to waves formed by wind.

24. A: Due to the earth's tilt on its axis, the two hemispheres experience different seasons at opposite times because when one is pointed toward the sun, the other is facing away. In the Northern Hemisphere, winter occurs in December and summer in July. In the Southern Hemisphere, it is the opposite. The two Equinoxes occur oppositely for each hemisphere as well.

25. B: The atomic number is equal to the number of protons in the nucleus, which is equal to the number of electrons. The number of protons plus the number of neutrons is equal to the mass number of the atom.

26. C: A parasite is an organism that feeds off the nutritional assets of another living thing called the host, which can lead to the host becoming malnourished or dying. Symbiosis occurs when there is a benefit to both organisms. A predator eats its prey. A producer produces food in the form of plant material that is eaten by a consumer.

27. C: In a pond, plants produce oxygen as a byproduct of photosynthesis. During eutrophication, plants die and decompose, causing increased levels of carbon dioxide. Fish cannot relocate from the pond, and they cannot live without oxygen, so they would die.

28. C: In an ecosystem, when one species is affected by overfishing or pollution, other species will either thrive due to a lack of competition or become extinct for the same reasons. The question states that the other species were not impacted by the overfishing or pollution. Thus, their populations would not have decreased for those reasons. Once extinct, the other species were no longer the potential prey of the Blue Pike or competing against them for similar food sources and so had the opportunity to increase their population numbers.

29. C: Human activities have not influenced the increased population of all species but have all played a role in the other environmental issues. As wetlands are degraded or lost, many ecosystems and species will also be lost, interrupting their respective food webs. Food webs within the actual oceans will also be reduced due to pollution and climate changes that impact water temperatures and levels. The diminishment of coral reefs means the ocean's water filtration system will be reduced or totally destroyed, affecting the ecosystems themselves as well as the organisms that use the area for breeding and feeding.

30. A: The large intestine's main function is the reabsorption of water into the body to form solid waste. It also allows for the absorption of vitamin K produced by microbes living inside the large intestine.

31. D: Digestion of food in the small intestine occurs by bile secreted by the liver. This is a chemical change.

32. C: The opposite moon phase of a new moon is a full moon. A new moon is the first moon phase, followed by the first quarter and then the full moon. The last moon is not a moon phase.

33. D: Species may theoretically be able to inhabit a particular area, called its fundamental niche. But the presence of competing species may mean that it only occupies part of its niche, called a realized niche.

34. C: In plants, all eggs and sperm are produced by gametophytes. In mosses, the gametophyte is the most prominent stage. In angiosperms, gametophytes are tiny and found inside anthers and pistils.

35. A: A triple beam balance would be used to measure the mass (in grams) of the gum in this experiment. An anemometer is used to measure wind speed. A hot plate is used to heat liquids. A microscope is used to magnify microscopic particles or organisms.

36. B: All of the answers use the System of International Units (SI) of measurement with the exception of gallons. A liter is the measurement of a liquid. Grams are a unit of measurement for the weight of an object, which would be measured on the triple beam balance. Meters measure length.

37. D: Operons are common in prokaryotes. They are units of DNA that control the transcription of DNA and code for their own regulatory proteins as well as structural proteins.

38. C: The independent variable is the variable that is changed in the experiment in order to determine its effect on the dependent variable or the outcome of the experiment. The dependent variable results from the experimenter making only one change to an experiment that can be repeated with the same results. Mrs. Jones's class was comparing the effects of sugar and artificial sweetener on the overall color of cookies once they are baked; thus, the one thing that should be changed in the experiment is the sugar and artificial sweetener in the recipe. All of the other ingredients stay the same. For the experiment to be valid and not influenced by any other variables, the students should keep the temperature and baking time the same, as these could affect the color of the cookies as well.

39. B: A decrease in a natural predator, such as a wolves, coyotes, bobcat, or wild dogs, would allow the population to become out of control. In a population of deer that has increased, there would be a natural decrease in a food source for the nutritional needs for the animals. Although deer have been known to share a human's developed habitat, it is often forced by reduced territory and food sources. An increase in hunting licenses would be used by local officials to try to control the population, helping to decrease the number of adults of breeding age.

40. D: An independent variable is a variable in the experiment that is changed by the experimenter. In this experiment, the class changed the type of solution that was applied to each of the plants in order to determine which would provide the most growth.

41. A: Since only 2 out of the initial 16 plants survived the whole month, it would be reasonable to test variables that were shared by all the plants. As such, the amount of liquid the plants need would be a good follow-up experiment. It is not specified as to which plants survived, so there is not enough information to think that testing the impact of salt is warranted. Additionally, since almost all the plants died, it is not reasonable to assume that a combination of the solutions would have an impact.

42. B: A control is a variable in the experiment that has not been changed by the experimenter but is subjected to the same processes as the other tested components. Plants are usually provided only water; these are being tested against bleach, salt, and diet soda, all of which are not regularly used to water a plant. The control acts as a reference point for comparison of the results.

43. D: A hypothesis is the use of prior knowledge in order to provide a hypothetical explanation for why something may or may not occur. A hypothesis can be proved wrong or right based on the results of the experiment and repeated trials.

44. C: In order to have accurate measurements, the use of a graduated cylinder would be best. A triple beam balance measures the weight of an object in grams. A flask and a test tube are used to contain a liquid while being heated or stored.

45. D: The first steps in a scientific investigation process involve asking a question about a problem and doing background research in order to determine if there is a valid reason for the question and whether it has been previously tested.

46. D: Although data from previous trials is important for the final lab report and results summary, it is not important for the current trial being tested. A final summary will incorporate all trial data results and observations in order to determine a final conclusion about the results. Temperature, color changes, and the production of a gas or odor indicate that a chemical change has occurred and should be recorded as an observation.

47. B: When working with flammable materials or an open flame, the accessible location of the fire blanket and extinguisher must be known in order to maintain safety. However, should the flames not go out immediately or spread too quickly, immediately leave the room and call 911. Close the door behind you in an effort to contain the fire.

48. C: The best graph to represent data from repeated trials of an experiment would be a line graph, as it would allow the viewer to see overlapping data without obstruction. The graph could be illustrated using different colors representing each trial or car, which would allow easy comparison.

49. B: The data tables compare the impact of the Northern and Southern Hemispheres on global warming with the overall changes globally, as seen in the top table. The Northern Hemisphere almost mirrors the results seen on the global table, while the Southern Hemisphere's table shows increases in temperature that are not as high as the Northern Hemispheres in years from 1980 to 2000. Most of the industrialized nations are found in the Northern Hemisphere. The Eastern and Western Hemispheres are not present on the table.

50. D: Blood is cooled as it passes through capillaries surrounding the sweat glands. Heat is absorbed along with excess salt and water and transferred to the glands as sweat. Droplets of sweat then evaporate from the skin surface to dissipate heat and cool the body. The kidney, bladder, and liver are not involved in regulating body temperature.

51. C: The most basic units of matter are protons, electrons, and neutrons. Protons are found in the nucleus, and have a positive charge. They are one of the three components of a helium atom a. When atoms have positive or negative charges, they are known as ions b. Molecules of oxygen, water, etc. d. are even more complex, consisting of one or more atoms held together by bonds.

52. D: Only cells with a membrane around the nucleus are called eukaryotes.

53. B: When Mario lets go of the book, he is no longer exerting any force on it, so he cannot be doing work on it. In all the other examples, Mario is exerting a force on the book in the direction that it is moving. In Answer A, Mario moves a book from the floor to the top shelf. Mario lifted up vertically on the book, in the same direction that the book moved, so he was doing work. In Answer C, Mario pushes a box of books across the room. This is also an example of work being done because the box moved in the direction of the force Mario applied. In Answer D, Mario is indirectly applying a horizontal force to the book because of the friction between the book and his head, so he is exerting a force on the book in the direction he is moving.

54. Third: All three laws of motion are operating, but the third law (forces come in equal and opposite pairs) best explains the motion. The first law (inertia) is shown from the fact that the balloon doesn't move until a force acts upon it. The second law (F = ma) is shown because you can see the force and the acceleration. The force comes from the contraction of the rubber balloon. The stretched rubber exerts a force on the air inside the balloon. This causes the air to accelerate in accordance with the second law. You can't see this acceleration because the air is invisible and because it is all the air in the room that the balloon is exerting a force on. However, the air in the room exerts an equal and opposite force on the balloon (this is Newton's third law), which causes the balloon to accelerate in the direction it did.

How to Overcome Test Anxiety

Just the thought of taking a test is enough to make most people a little nervous. A test is an important event that can have a long-term impact on your future, so it's important to take it seriously and it's natural to feel anxious about performing well. But just because anxiety is normal, that doesn't mean that it's helpful in test taking, or that you should simply accept it as part of your life. Anxiety can have a variety of effects. These effects can be mild, like making you feel slightly nervous, or severe, like blocking your ability to focus or remember even a simple detail.

If you experience test anxiety—whether severe or mild—it's important to know how to beat it. To discover this, first you need to understand what causes test anxiety.

Causes of Test Anxiety

While we often think of anxiety as an uncontrollable emotional state, it can actually be caused by simple, practical things. One of the most common causes of test anxiety is that a person does not feel adequately prepared for their test. This feeling can be the result of many different issues such as poor study habits or lack of organization, but the most common culprit is time management. Starting to study too late, failing to organize your study time to cover all of the material, or being distracted while you study will mean that you're not well prepared for the test. This may lead to cramming the night before, which will cause you to be physically and mentally exhausted for the test. Poor time management also contributes to feelings of stress, fear, and hopelessness as you realize you are not well prepared but don't know what to do about it.

Other times, test anxiety is not related to your preparation for the test but comes from unresolved fear. This may be a past failure on a test, or poor performance on tests in general. It may come from comparing yourself to others who seem to be performing better or from the stress of living up to expectations. Anxiety may be driven by fears of the future—how failure on this test would affect your educational and career goals. These fears are often completely irrational, but they can still negatively impact your test performance.

Elements of Test Anxiety

As mentioned earlier, test anxiety is considered to be an emotional state, but it has physical and mental components as well. Sometimes you may not even realize that you are suffering from test anxiety until you notice the physical symptoms. These can include trembling hands, rapid heartbeat, sweating, nausea, and tense muscles. Extreme anxiety may lead to fainting or vomiting. Obviously, any of these symptoms can have a negative impact on testing. It is important to recognize them as soon as they begin to occur so that you can address the problem before it damages your performance.

The mental components of test anxiety include trouble focusing and inability to remember learned information. During a test, your mind is on high alert, which can help you recall information and stay focused for an extended period of time. However, anxiety interferes with your mind's natural processes, causing you to blank out, even on the questions you know well. The strain of testing during anxiety makes it difficult to stay focused, especially on a test that may take several hours. Extreme anxiety can take a huge mental toll, making it difficult not only to recall test information but even to understand the test questions or pull your thoughts together.

Effects of Test Anxiety

Test anxiety is like a disease—if left untreated, it will get progressively worse. Anxiety leads to poor performance, and this reinforces the feelings of fear and failure, which in turn lead to poor performances on subsequent tests. It can grow from a mild nervousness to a crippling condition. If allowed to progress, test anxiety can have a big impact on your schooling, and consequently on your future.

Test anxiety can spread to other parts of your life. Anxiety on tests can become anxiety in any stressful situation, and blanking on a test can turn into panicking in a job situation. But fortunately, you don't have to let anxiety rule your testing and determine your grades. There are a number of relatively simple steps you can take to move past anxiety and function normally on a test and in the rest of life.

Physical Steps for Beating Test Anxiety

While test anxiety is a serious problem, the good news is that it can be overcome. It doesn't have to control your ability to think and remember information. While it may take time, you can begin taking steps today to beat anxiety.

Just as your first hint that you may be struggling with anxiety comes from the physical symptoms, the first step to treating it is also physical. Rest is crucial for having a clear, strong mind. If you are tired, it is much easier to give in to anxiety. But if you establish good sleep habits, your body and mind will be ready to perform optimally, without the strain of exhaustion. Additionally, sleeping well helps you to retain information better, so you're more likely to recall the answers when you see the test questions.

Getting good sleep means more than going to bed on time. It's important to allow your brain time to relax. Take study breaks from time to time so it doesn't get overworked, and don't study right before bed. Take time to rest your mind before trying to rest your body, or you may find it difficult to fall asleep.

Along with sleep, other aspects of physical health are important in preparing for a test. Good nutrition is vital for good brain function. Sugary foods and drinks may give a burst of energy but this burst is followed by a crash, both physically and emotionally. Instead, fuel your body with protein and vitamin-rich foods.

Also, drink plenty of water. Dehydration can lead to headaches and exhaustion, especially if your brain is already under stress from the rigors of the test. Particularly if your test is a long one, drink water during the breaks. And if possible, take an energy-boosting snack to eat between sections.

Along with sleep and diet, a third important part of physical health is exercise. Maintaining a steady workout schedule is helpful, but even taking 5-minute study breaks to walk can help get your blood pumping faster and clear your head. Exercise also releases endorphins, which contribute to a positive feeling and can help combat test anxiety.

When you nurture your physical health, you are also contributing to your mental health. If your body is healthy, your mind is much more likely to be healthy as well. So take time to rest, nourish your body with healthy food and water, and get moving as much as possible. Taking these physical steps will make you stronger and more able to take the mental steps necessary to overcome test anxiety.

Mental Steps for Beating Test Anxiety

Working on the mental side of test anxiety can be more challenging, but as with the physical side, there are clear steps you can take to overcome it. As mentioned earlier, test anxiety often stems from lack of preparation, so the obvious solution is to prepare for the test. Effective studying may be the most important weapon you have for beating test anxiety, but you can and should employ several other mental tools to combat fear.

First, boost your confidence by reminding yourself of past success—tests or projects that you aced. If you're putting as much effort into preparing for this test as you did for those, there's no reason you should expect to fail here. Work hard to prepare; then trust your preparation.

Second, surround yourself with encouraging people. It can be helpful to find a study group, but be sure that the people you're around will encourage a positive attitude. If you spend time with others who are anxious or cynical, this will only contribute to your own anxiety. Look for others who are motivated to study hard from a desire to succeed, not from a fear of failure.

Third, reward yourself. A test is physically and mentally tiring, even without anxiety, and it can be helpful to have something to look forward to. Plan an activity following the test, regardless of the outcome, such as going to a movie or getting ice cream.

When you are taking the test, if you find yourself beginning to feel anxious, remind yourself that you know the material. Visualize successfully completing the test. Then take a few deep, relaxing breaths and return to it. Work through the questions carefully but with confidence, knowing that you are capable of succeeding.

Developing a healthy mental approach to test taking will also aid in other areas of life. Test anxiety affects more than just the actual test—it can be damaging to your mental health and even contribute to depression. It's important to beat test anxiety before it becomes a problem for more than testing.

Study Strategy

Being prepared for the test is necessary to combat anxiety, but what does being prepared look like? You may study for hours on end and still not feel prepared. What you need is a strategy for test prep. The next few pages outline our recommended steps to help you plan out and conquer the challenge of preparation.

Step 1: Scope Out the Test

Learn everything you can about the format (multiple choice, essay, etc.) and what will be on the test. Gather any study materials, course outlines, or sample exams that may be available. Not only will this help you to prepare, but knowing what to expect can help to alleviate test anxiety.

Step 2: Map Out the Material

Look through the textbook or study guide and make note of how many chapters or sections it has. Then divide these over the time you have. For example, if a book has 15 chapters and you have five days to study, you need to cover three chapters each day. Even better, if you have the time, leave an extra day at the end for overall review after you have gone through the material in depth.

If time is limited, you may need to prioritize the material. Look through it and make note of which sections you think you already have a good grasp on, and which need review. While you are studying, skim quickly through the familiar sections and take more time on the challenging parts.

Write out your plan so you don't get lost as you go. Having a written plan also helps you feel more in control of the study, so anxiety is less likely to arise from feeling overwhelmed at the amount to cover.

Step 3: Gather Your Tools

Decide what study method works best for you. Do you prefer to highlight in the book as you study and then go back over the highlighted portions? Or do you type out notes of the important information? Or is it helpful to make flashcards that you can carry with you? Assemble the pens, index cards, highlighters, post-it notes, and any other materials you may need so you won't be distracted by getting up to find things while you study.

If you're having a hard time retaining the information or organizing your notes, experiment with different methods. For example, try color-coding by subject with colored pens, highlighters, or post-it notes. If you learn better by hearing, try recording yourself reading your notes so you can listen while in the car, working out, or simply sitting at your desk. Ask a friend to quiz you from your flashcards, or try teaching someone the material to solidify it in your mind.

Step 4: Create Your Environment

It's important to avoid distractions while you study. This includes both the obvious distractions like visitors and the subtle distractions like an uncomfortable chair (or a too-comfortable couch that makes you want to fall asleep). Set up the best study environment possible: good lighting and a comfortable work area. If background music helps you focus, you may want to turn it on, but otherwise keep the room quiet. If you are using a computer to take notes, be sure you don't have any other windows open, especially applications like social media, games, or anything else that could distract you. Silence your phone and turn off notifications. Be sure to keep water close by so you stay hydrated while you study (but avoid unhealthy drinks and snacks).

Also, take into account the best time of day to study. Are you freshest first thing in the morning? Try to set aside some time then to work through the material. Is your mind clearer in the afternoon or evening? Schedule your study session then. Another method is to study at the same time of day that you will take the test, so that your brain gets used to working on the material at that time and will be ready to focus at test time.

Step 5: Study!

Once you have done all the study preparation, it's time to settle into the actual studying. Sit down, take a few moments to settle your mind so you can focus, and begin to follow your study plan. Don't give in to distractions or let yourself procrastinate. This is your time to prepare so you'll be ready to fearlessly approach the test. Make the most of the time and stay focused.

Of course, you don't want to burn out. If you study too long you may find that you're not retaining the information very well. Take regular study breaks. For example, taking five minutes out of every hour to walk briskly, breathing deeply and swinging your arms, can help your mind stay fresh.

As you get to the end of each chapter or section, it's a good idea to do a quick review. Remind yourself of what you learned and work on any difficult parts. When you feel that you've mastered the material, move on to the next part. At the end of your study session, briefly skim through your notes again.

But while review is helpful, cramming last minute is NOT. If at all possible, work ahead so that you won't need to fit all your study into the last day. Cramming overloads your brain with more information than it can process and retain, and your tired mind may struggle to recall even previously learned information when it is overwhelmed with last-minute study. Also, the urgent nature of cramming and the stress placed on your brain contribute to anxiety. You'll be more likely to go to the test feeling unprepared and having trouble thinking clearly.

So don't cram, and don't stay up late before the test, even just to review your notes at a leisurely pace. Your brain needs rest more than it needs to go over the information again. In fact, plan to finish your studies by noon or early afternoon the day before the test. Give your brain the rest of the day to relax or focus on other things, and get a good night's sleep. Then you will be fresh for the test and better able to recall what you've studied.

Step 6: Take a Practice Test

Many courses offer sample tests, either online or in the study materials. This is an excellent resource to check whether you have mastered the material, as well as to prepare for the test format and environment.

Check the test format ahead of time: the number of questions, the type (multiple choice, free response, etc.), and the time limit. Then create a plan for working through them. For example, if you have 30 minutes to take a 60-question test, your limit is 30 seconds per question. Spend less time on the questions you know well so that you can take more time on the difficult ones.

If you have time to take several practice tests, take the first one open book, with no time limit. Work through the questions at your own pace and make sure you fully understand them. Gradually work up to taking a test under test conditions: sit at a desk with all study materials put away and set a timer. Pace yourself to make sure you finish the test with time to spare and go back to check your answers if you have time.

After each test, check your answers. On the questions you missed, be sure you understand why you missed them. Did you misread the question (tests can use tricky wording)? Did you forget the information? Or was it something you hadn't learned? Go back and study any shaky areas that the practice tests reveal.

Taking these tests not only helps with your grade, but also aids in combating test anxiety. If you're already used to the test conditions, you're less likely to worry about it, and working through tests until you're scoring well gives you a confidence boost. Go through the practice tests until you feel comfortable, and then you can go into the test knowing that you're ready for it.

Test Tips

On test day, you should be confident, knowing that you've prepared well and are ready to answer the questions. But aside from preparation, there are several test day strategies you can employ to maximize your performance.

First, as stated before, get a good night's sleep the night before the test (and for several nights before that, if possible). Go into the test with a fresh, alert mind rather than staying up late to study.

Try not to change too much about your normal routine on the day of the test. It's important to eat a nutritious breakfast, but if you normally don't eat breakfast at all, consider eating just a protein bar. If you're a coffee drinker, go ahead and have your normal coffee. Just make sure you time it so that the caffeine doesn't wear off right in the middle of your test. Avoid sugary beverages, and drink enough water to stay hydrated but not so much that you need a restroom break 10 minutes into the test. If your test isn't first thing in the morning, consider going for a walk or doing a light workout before the test to get your blood flowing.

Allow yourself enough time to get ready, and leave for the test with plenty of time to spare so you won't have the anxiety of scrambling to arrive in time. Another reason to be early is to select a good seat. It's helpful to sit away from doors and windows, which can be distracting. Find a good seat, get out your supplies, and settle your mind before the test begins.

When the test begins, start by going over the instructions carefully, even if you already know what to expect. Make sure you avoid any careless mistakes by following the directions.

Then begin working through the questions, pacing yourself as you've practiced. If you're not sure on an answer, don't spend too much time on it, and don't let it shake your confidence. Either skip it and come back later, or eliminate as many wrong answers as possible and guess among the remaining ones. Don't dwell on these questions as you continue—put them out of your mind and focus on what lies ahead.

Be sure to read all of the answer choices, even if you're sure the first one is the right answer. Sometimes you'll find a better one if you keep reading. But don't second-guess yourself if you do immediately know the answer. Your gut instinct is usually right. Don't let test anxiety rob you of the information you know.

If you have time at the end of the test (and if the test format allows), go back and review your answers. Be cautious about changing any, since your first instinct tends to be correct, but make sure you didn't misread any of the questions or accidentally mark the wrong answer choice. Look over any you skipped and make an educated guess.

At the end, leave the test feeling confident. You've done your best, so don't waste time worrying about your performance or wishing you could change anything. Instead, celebrate the successful completion of this test. And finally, use this test to learn how to deal with anxiety even better next time.

Review Video: Test Anxiety
Visit mometrix.com/academy and enter code: 100340

Important Qualification

Not all anxiety is created equal. If your test anxiety is causing major issues in your life beyond the classroom or testing center, or if you are experiencing troubling physical symptoms related to your anxiety, it may be a sign of a serious physiological or psychological condition. If this sounds like your situation, we strongly encourage you to seek professional help.

Thank You

We at Mometrix would like to extend our heartfelt thanks to you, our friend and patron, for allowing us to play a part in your journey. It is a privilege to serve people from all walks of life who are unified in their commitment to building the best future they can for themselves.

The preparation you devote to these important testing milestones may be the most valuable educational opportunity you have for making a real difference in your life. We encourage you to put your heart into it—that feeling of succeeding, overcoming, and yes, conquering will be well worth the hours you've invested.

We want to hear your story, your struggles and your successes, and if you see any opportunities for us to improve our materials so we can help others even more effectively in the future, please share that with us as well. **The team at Mometrix would be absolutely thrilled to hear from you!** So please, send us an email (support@mometrix.com) and let's stay in touch.

If you'd like some additional help, check out these other resources we offer for your exam:

http://MometrixFlashcards.com/MCA

Online Resources

Due to our efforts to try to keep this book to a manageable length, we've created a link that will give you access to all of your online resources:

mometrix.com/resources719/ssmcag8sci

It's Your Moment, Let's Celebrate It!

Share your story @mometrixtestpreparation